✠ FOOLS ✠
FOR CHRIST:

FIFTY
DIVINE ECCENTRIC
ARTISTS,
MARTYRS,
STIGMATISTS,
AND
UNSUNG SAINTS

BY HEATHER KING

Published by Holy Hell Books
www.heather-king.com

Cover and interior design by DoubleMRanch.com
Published in the United States of America
ISBN 978-0578512822

"The only real sadness, the only real failure,

the only great tragedy in life,

is not to become a saint."

—LÉON BLOY

TABLE OF CONTENTS

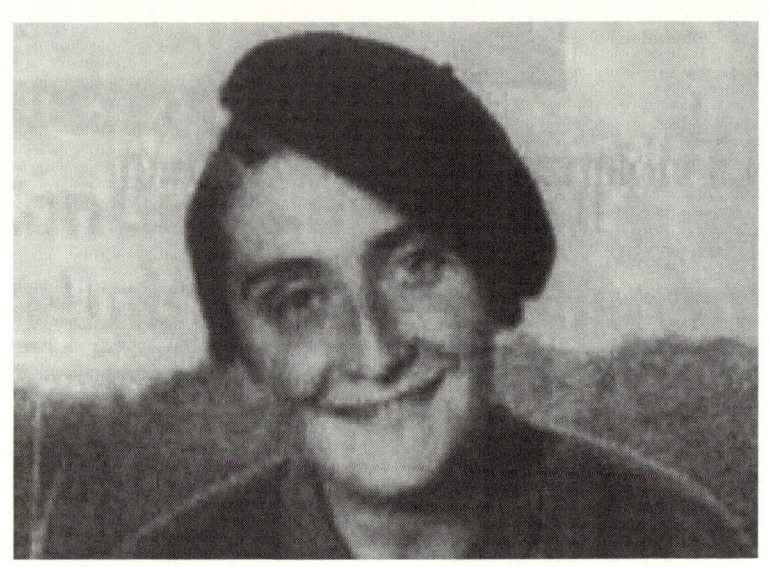

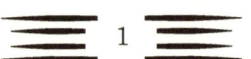 1

SERVANT OF GOD
MADELEINE DELBRÊL

Madeleine Delbrêl (1904-1964), French convert, social
activist, and mystic, founded an experimental lay community
dedicated to social justice and the works of mercy.

In her youth Delbrêl, an only child, was resolutely atheistic.
After converting in 1924, she became engaged to a man
who broke off their relationship to join the Dominicans. Then
her father went blind. The experiences devastated her.

In 1933, she accepted the offer from a priest of a two-
bedroom house in the largely Communist Paris suburb of
Ivry-sur-Seine. Along with two other women, she moved
in shortly thereafter. Raspail, as their house was known,
became a hub of social and political activism with an
emphasis on treating Christ in "the least of these" with
humility, verve, and humor.

The community members befriended the Communists
among whom they lived. Over the years, Raspail sheltered
incorrigible drunks, borderline personalities, and families
spilling over with children. Delbrêl was dazzled by the notion
that authentic freedom is grounded in Christ, and she also
wrote of the Church's failure to adequately love the outcast
and the prisoner.

Though she resisted what she called "literature," she constantly scribbled pamphlets, letters-to-the-editor, and tracts.

Her books include *We, the Ordinary People of the Streets*, *The Little Monk*, and *The Joy of Believing*. "When you finally discover that you are just one of the little people, don't conclude that this makes you special." "The Gospel is not meant to be read by us, but to be received within us."

She worked indefatigably during WWII to welcome refugees, arrange housing, and console the traumatized. All the while she smoked like a fiend, wore salvaged pillbox hats decorated with fake flowers, and took abysmal care of her health.

In time, she traveled to Switzerland, Scotland, Africa, Poland, and Rome. She resisted organizing Raspail as a "Pious Institute" with fixed rules and regulations, as was decreed by the Vatican for lay organizations in 1947. She believed in "people without categories" and in a life without boundaries.

Pope Francis has called the laity to "the outskirts of existence." At the same time, "[The layperson] is to create and sow hope, to proclaim the faith, not from a pulpit but from his everyday life." Delbrêl is a wonderful exemplar. We, too, are called to "the outskirts" by living among people who have turned their backs on God. We, too, are called to sow hope in the alien and the stranger, whether or not they share our faith.

On October 13, 1964, Delbrêl was working, as usual, at the battered desk from which she ministered to her "tiny multitude." A community member found her lifeless body late that afternoon.

She wrote: "Each time that we are torn apart because we choose to be faithful to God's faithfulness to us, we become as it were breaches in the world's resistance."

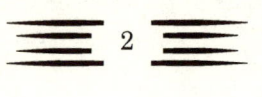

GERARD MANLEY HOPKINS

Gerard Manley Hopkins (1844-1889), an English convert to Roman Catholicism and a Jesuit priest, produced some of the most complex, astonishing, and wrenching poetry of our age.

In 1886, the Irish poet Kathleen Tynan asked why a man so drawn to beauty and art had decided to become a priest. Hopkins replied: "You wouldn't give only the dull ones to Almighty God."

Hopkins was in all worldly senses a failure. His family nearly disowned him when he converted from Anglicanism. He was melancholy, sickly, small and pale. When the Jesuits transferred him to Dublin, he felt a stranger as an Englishman in Ireland; a stranger among his closest friends, none of whom saw or encouraged his brilliance; and a stranger in his own skin. He suffered conflict, depression, darkness, and doubt. He was an ineffective teacher of Latin and Greek (his job at University College Dublin) and a feckless priest. In 1884 he began a series now known as "The Terrible Sonnets." Only a handful of his poems were published in his lifetime.

"What is my wretched life?" he wrote in his notes after a retreat, the year before he died. "Five wasted years almost have passed in Ireland. I am ashamed of the little I have done, of my waste of time, although my helplessness and weakness is such that I could scarcely do otherwise...All my undertakings miscarry: I am like a straining eunuch. I wish then for death; yet if I died now I should die imperfect, no master of myself, and that is the worst failure of all. O my God, look down on me."

Yet always, in the midst of despair, Hopkins offers a stab of hope. "What is all this juice and all this joy?" he wrote of spring. "God's Grandeur" (1877) ends in a choking sob of exultation.:

> *"And for all this, nature is never spent;*
> *There lives the dearest freshness deep down things;*
> *And though the last lights off the black West went*
> *Oh, morning, at the brown brink eastward, springs—*
> *Because the Holy Ghost over the bent*
> *World broods with warm breast and with ah! bright wings."*

"Inscape" was his term for the indwelling individuality of people and things; an impression of God's presence in the world. Later he would find corroboration in Duns Scotus

(1270-1308), who held that every physical thing carries within it the reason why it is unique unto itself; different from every other thing. He utilized—in fact, claimed to have discovered—"sprung rhythm," a poetic meter that aims to imitate human speech.

For those of us who love him, the very titles of his poems—"The Wind-Hover," "To Seem the Stranger," "Pied Beauty"—shake us out "like shook foil." They "adazzle" our souls. They send our roots rain.

His fidelity to his vows, his bearing of the tension of celibacy, his loneliness and exile exploded into rare and precious fruit. "All things counter, original, spare, strange"—a line from "Pied Beauty"—describes our lives in Christ; describes him.

He died at 44 of complications from typhus. His last words were: "I am so happy, I am so happy, I loved my life."

LÉON BLOY

Léon Bloy (1846-1917), French novelist, poet, and fervent Catholic convert, had a notoriously foul temper, alienated many of his fellow literati, and burned with love for Christ. A ranter-writer, he refused to get a day job, was perpetually penniless, and at one point fell violently in love with a prostitute who later converted, saw visions, and was committed to an insane asylum.

Bloy eventually married and had four children, two of whom died in infancy because of his inability, or refusal, to earn a living. He railed, "Money is the blood of the poor." He described himself as "in fellowship of impatience with all the rebels, all the disappointed, all the thwarted, all the damned of this world."

And he felt to the bone the workings of the Mystical Body of Christ. In *Pilgrim of the Absolute*, for example, a collection of diary entries, he wrote:

Every man who begets a free act projects his personality into the infinite…If he begets an impure act, he perhaps darkens thousands of hearts whom he does not know, who are mysteriously linked to him, and who need this man to be pure as a traveler dying of thirst needs the Gospel's draught of water. A charitable act, an impulse of real pity sings for him the divine praises, from the time of Adam to the end of the ages; it cures the sick, consoles those in despair, calms storms, ransoms prisoners, converts the infidel and protects mankind.

From a man who committed many such sins himself paradoxically came this beautiful apologia for the teachings of the Church on, among other things, sex. We try to be pure because someone else needs us to be pure. Someone in pain needs us to refrain from using another, whether in reality or fantasy, to anaesthetize our own pain. Maybe that person is standing in front of us in line at the grocery store with ADD, three screaming kids and her dingy food stamps scattered all over the check-out counter. Maybe that person is our spouse. Maybe that person is the child who has been touched, maybe by a priest, and is going to grow up wanting to inappropriately touch someone else: someone younger, someone weaker.

"Everything that happens to me calls for adoration": this from a man who suffered torments of impatience, loneliness, and humiliating poverty his whole life. The parable of the shepherd who left the ninety-nine behind to go in search of the one was especially dear to Bloy, a lost sheep himself. "There's one thing the Church has always taught and which is the teaching of all saints, without exception. It is that the salvation of one soul matters more than bodily help given to a hundred thousand poor men. This is not defined in dogmatic form; but it is so linked to the essential Doctrine, to the Word of God, that is impossible to be a Christian if you doubt it."

Bloy was a loyal, dogged friend. He came to discover that, at a certain height, joy and sorrow are the same thing. He died at the age of seventy-one, knowing what we would all do well to remember: "There is only one sadness; it is the sadness of NOT BEING SAINTS."

 4

CARYLL HOUSELANDER

Caryll Houselander (1901-1954), British mystic, poet and spiritual teacher, wore a pair of big round tortoiseshell glasses, lived in London during the Blitz, and until she died at 53 from breast cancer, apparently barely slept or ate. A friend observed: "She used to cover her face with some abominable chalky-white substance which gave it quite often the tragic look one associates with clowns and great comedians."

That Divine Eccentric, Maisie Ward's fine biography, charts Houselander's difficult childhood, her reversion to the Church in 1925, and her unrequited love for a British spy who would be the model for Ian Fleming's "James Bond." She had an eclectic coterie of friends and was utterly devoted to Christ. She never married.

Ward writes, "The sure cure for bitterness, Caryll comments, is to pray and do penance for the person: love will grow in proportion. 'It is not according to how much penance I do or how many prayers I say, but how much love I put into it.'"

Houselander was not perfect. She swore and drank. She had a sharp tongue. And she was a wonderful storyteller.

> *"I was running someone down [to a priest], saying beastly things of him. Suddenly I noticed that [the priest's] eyes were shut. 'You are not listening,' I said. He replied, 'I cannot—not to that; you see we are both present at the Mass. Whilst you were trying to make me think ill of X, Christ our Lord was offering Himself up to God to redeem them.'*
>
> *'But we are not at Mass,' I said...and he said, 'When your thoughts are hard or bitter or sad, let the sanctuary bell silence them. It is always ringing.' "*

She became a prolific and popular author. Her works include *The Reed of God, A Rocking-Horse Catholic*, and *The Risen Christ. Guilt* (1951) contains passages on the mental suffering, among others, of serial killer Peter Kürten ("The Monster of Düsseldorf"), Hans Christian Andersen, Rimbaud, and St. Thérèse of Lisieux.

Houselander suffered greatly: from poverty, from frail health, from neuroses. She had a life-long and especially deep and tender bond with traumatized children, and loved teaching them how to draw, paint, and carve small animals out of wood.

The novelist F. Scott Fitzgerald once famously observed, "The test of a first-rate intelligence is the ability to hold two opposed ideas in the mind at the same time, and still retain the ability to function."

Perhaps the test of a first-rate *heart* is the ability to connect two ideas that, while not necessarily opposed, are seemingly unrelated.

For instance, these two quotes from Houselander:

"I am sure, as never before, that the Russian idea of Christ, humble, suffering, and crowned with thorns is the only true one; that it is impossible to be a Christian unless the humility of poverty of Christ is taken literally and all that tends towards power, grandeur, success and so on, is avoided and despised."

and

"I think all teddy bears need knitted suits."

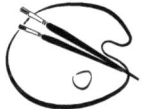

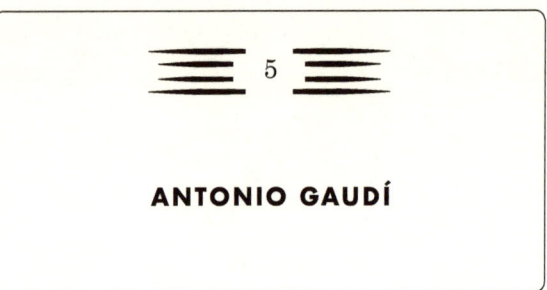

5

ANTONIO GAUDÍ

Antoni Gaudí (1852-1926), Catalan, designed and built La Sagrada Familia, perhaps the world's most well-known church. He has been called Barcelona's "priest of beauty," "God's architect," and a madman.

His biographer, Gijs van Hensbergen, observed: "Gaudí is a very contemporary figure—holistic, spiritual and astonishingly original. He was an ecologist: recycling broken tiles, crockery, children's toys, old needles from textile mills, metal bands for baling cotton cloth, bedsprings and the burnt-out linings of industrial ovens to create his buildings." He adds, "Some of [Gaudí's] work has a Disney-fied vulgarity."

After a failed love affair in his youth, Gaudí remained celibate for the rest of his life. He became a vegetarian, subsisting largely on lettuce leaves dipped in milk, nuts, and dried fruit. He was arrogant, stubborn, and convinced of his own genius. He once told a reporter, "Men may be divided into two types: men of words and men of action. The first speak; the latter act. I am of the second group."

Gaudí achieved great fame. He also knew much heartache, including the deaths of his beloved father (1906) and his alcoholic niece Rosa (1912). He worked continually and drove his employees mercilessly. A devout Catholic, he attended daily confession and daily Mass.

He designed lampposts, newsstands, mansions, and the urban development project Park Güell. But his undisputed masterpiece is the Sagrada Familia, his church in Barcelona that has been under intermittent construction since 1882.

Inspired by nature, he transcended the Gothic, brought the catenary arch to new heights, and envisioned a church as the construction of a forest, with massive columns standing in for trees, and "branches" supporting a structure of hyperboloid vaults. The craftsmanship, design, sculptures, four-armed crosses, ceramic mosaics, stained glass, and almost berserk ornamentation perhaps have to be seen to be believed. From 1915 on, he devoted himself exclusively to the Sagrada Familia.

Fiercely private, he never taught and rarely committed his thoughts to paper. He prayed and fasted, sometimes to the point of endangering his health. By the last years of his life, he was nearly destitute. He walked the streets begging money to continue construction on what had come to be known as the Cathedral of the Poor. It was as if he had slowly allowed the church to consume him. The poorer, the older, the sicker, the more invisible Gaudi became, the taller, the more beautiful, mysterious, and indescribably sublime became the Sagrada Familia.

By 1925, he had moved into his studio and actually lived at the church. On June 7, 1926, he was struck on his way to Confession by a tramcar driver whose driver mistook him for a drunken tramp. He died in the charity ward, gripping a crucifix, murmuring "Jesus, Déu meu!" (My God!)

He was buried in the crypt of the Sagrada Familia. His gravestone, translated, reads in part: "Henceforth the ashes of this great man await the resurrection of the dead."

Construction continues. And Gaudí lives on.

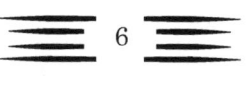

6

VENERABLE
MATT TALBOT

Matt Talbot (1856-1925), patron of struggling and recovering addicts and alcoholics, was born to a working-class Catholic family in Dublin, the second oldest of twelve children. Times were hard: his father was an alcoholic and the Irish Potato Famine had recently ended. As a youth, he quit school to work and, by the age of 13, was drinking alcoholically himself.

By the time he'd reached his twenties, even Talbot's own mates refused to stand him drinks. Then one day, scrounging for money to squander at the pub, he stole the violin of a blind street busker. His conscience stricken, he put down the booze and began to live a quiet, hidden life of penitence and prayer. He was 28.

He became a Third Order Franciscan. Each day he quietly attended early morning Mass, then went to his job on the docks. In *Matt Talbot*, journalist Eddie Doherty tells of the bitter rancor between workers and management at the time.

There were bloody riots, assassinations, Irish heroes, British villains. A member of the Irish Transport and General Workers Union, Talbot struck with his co-workers after the Dublin Lockout of 1913, but declined to comment further.

When he was himself arrested by the British for questioning, forced to raise his hands against a wall, and stand, by some accounts for hours, his response was: "God is so good. Isn't it a pity more men do not love Him." He was said to be "happy little man . . . who smiled at everything except a dirty joke."

Through it all he fasted, prayed, gave alms. He sustained himself for hard physical labor with dry crusts of bread and a ghastly concoction of cold tea and cocoa. His bed consisted of two rough pine planks with a log for a pillow. He allowed himself only three and a half hours of sleep per night. He rose at two, prayed for two hours, then went and knelt outside the local Jesuit church, knees bare, thin overcoat flapping in the wind, and waited for the doors to open at six. After Mass, he went to work for the day. If he managed to scrape together a few extra coins, he gave them away or sent them to the missions

With a special devotion to the Blessed Mother, he began secretly to bind his body with heavy chains: a symbol of his desire to be a slave to Mary.

Talbot died on a Dublin street, walking to Mass, on June 7, 1925. Chains and cords were found wrapped around his body. Some were embedded in his flesh.

Ten years later New York stockbroker Bill Wilson and Dr. Bob Smith, hopeless drunks both, met for the first time. The two went on to found Alcoholics Anonymous, an organization that, since 1939, has by all accounts helped millions of alcoholics and addicts worlwide to achieve and maintain sobriety. AA, whose only requirement for membership is a desire to stop drinking, doesn't remotely suggest rising at 2 to pray, daily Mass, fasting, or the wearing of chains.

Yet perhaps those austerities were necessary. Perhaps one man—truly anonymous during his lifetime—had to be so appalled by the hurt he had caused, so grateful to be sober, that he prayed and did penance every remaining second of his life. Perhaps one man had to love God as much as Matt Talbot did to pave the way for the soul-sick, desperately lonely drunks who came after. Perhaps a Dublin saint lived in solitude for forty years so that a world-wide fellowship could be born.

"I will make you fishers of men," Christ told the disciples: perhaps it's no accident that Talbot spent so much of his life on the Dublin docks. In *Story of Matt Talbot*, Malachy Gerard Carroll imagines Matt "standing on the wharf, head bent, to the chimes and the cry of the sea gulls around him, his figure one with the dust and the grime, and the oily waters." He imagines "heat and sweat and dust and scummy water...a thing of beauty...lifted into the presence of the Holy Trinity."

IRENA SENDLER

Irena Sendler (1910-2008), Polish Catholic social worker and a candidate for the 2007 Nobel Peace Prize, is credited with saving 2500 Jewish children by smuggling them from the Warsaw Ghetto and establishing them in individual and group homes.

Sendler's father, a doctor with humanitarian ideals, died when Sendler was seven from typhus contracted while treating poor Jewish patients.

When WW II began, Sendler was a 29-year-old social worker and a third of her city's population were Jews: hounded, beaten, starved, herded into the infamous Warsaw Ghetto.

"In 1939 when the Germans invaded, Poland was drowning in a sea of blood," Sendler observed. "And it was the Jewish children who suffered the most."

Though aiding a Jew was subject to the death penalty, an extraordinary resistance movement formed, consisting of

Polish Democrats and other Catholic activists who carried out the perilous work of providing food, shelter, and forged documents. The Council for Aid to Jews, known by its code name, Zegota, selected Sendler as the head of its Children's Bureau.

When the Nazis began transporting Jews to the death camps, Jewish parents faced an unthinkable decision: should they bring their children or leave them behind? Sendler volunteered to take many of them, assign new identities, and arrange for adoption by non-Jewish families. Though Catholicism was also a target of the Nazis, many convents and monasteries also willingly took and cared for such children. Sendler and her co-workers wrote the true identities of the children on rolls of paper, placed the rolls in jars, and buried them.

She was arrested by the Gestapo on October 20, 1943, incarcerated at Pawiak Prison, and over a period of three months, tortured. Her interrogators broke her feet and legs, crippling her for life, but she never divulged the names of either her collaborators or the hidden children.

She was saved from execution when a friend bribed a guard; then, after her release, immediately continued her resistance from hiding. After the war, she married and had two children. For decades, she lived a modest, anonymous life in Warsaw.

Fifty-five years later and a continent away, a different set of children found her. In 1999, an American teacher named Norman Conrad helped his students to discover and research Irena Sendler. They wrote a play, "Life in a Jar," that has been staged throughout the U.S. and Europe, and established a foundation to promulgate Sendler's message.

In 2007, she was nominated to receive the Nobel Peace Prize. "I'm sure I have many faults," she observed in the PBS documentary *Irena Sendler: In the Name of Their Mothers* (2011), "but there's one thing I can boast about. I'm a good organizer."

Her modesty was remarkable. In her autobiography, she observed, "This constant emphasis on how extraordinary our work was – it is uncomfortable. A Jew, a Frenchman, a German, they are, after all, the same people, like us – that was the only thought in our minds. That which we did came from a need in our hearts."

 8

**SERVANT OF GOD
FATHER WALTER CISZEK**

Fr. Walter Ciszek, sj (1904-1984) was born to a large
Polish Catholic family in the mining town of Shenandoah,
Pennsylvania. As a youth he headed up a street gang and
proved so incorrigible that his father once went to the police
and asked them to put young Ciszek in reform school.

nstead, mulishly stubborn, he developed a private, secret
desire to be a Jesuit priest. He was accepted into seminary,
studied in Rome, and was ordained in 1937. He felt a
passionate call to go to Russia, but was instead assigned to
Albertin in eastern Poland.

When the Russians invaded and closed the Jesuit mission
down, Fr. Ciszek, with permission from his order, snuck
across the Russian border. There, he worked in a lumber
camp for a year: learning the language, quietly performing
baptisms, absolutions, and anointings, and—some of
the happiest moments of his life, he would later recall—
celebrating clandestine Masses in the woods with a
priest friend.

Arrested one night on phony charges of being a Vatican spy,
he was sent to the notorious Lubianka Prison. Much of his
five years there was spent in solitary confinement. In *He
Leadeth Me*, the spiritual classic he later wrote of that time,

he told of praying that the Holy Spirit would provide a clever retort to put his interrogators smartly in their place. Instead, in one particularly grueling session, he finally and numbly signed page after page of a trumped-up "confession."

Back in his cell, he was devastated. He, who had prided himself on his strength, had succumbed. It struck with the force of revelation: for all his prayer and self-discipline, he had still been relying largely on himself. The episode was a "purgatory" that left him "cleansed to the bone" and marked a turning point after which he abandoned himself completely to God's will.

He was sentenced to fifteen years of hard labor at a Siberian work camp. In the sub-arctic cold, and under penalty of death, he and his fellow believers secretly celebrated daily Mass during lunch break: "[T]hese men would actually fast all day long and do exhausting physical labor without a bite to eat since dinner the evening before, just to be able to receive the Holy Eucharist—that was how much the Sacrament meant to them in this otherwise God-forsaken place."

Released from Siberia in 1955, he worked as an auto mechanic and served as village priest. In 1963 he was exchanged for two Soviet spies and, after twenty-three years,

Fr. Ciszek came home. The spirit still shone through his blue eyes, yet "in many ways, I am almost a stranger."

This mischievous Pole, tender of heart and tough as nails, evokes another saint: Thérèse of Lisieux. Both were fiercely sure of their vocations; both underwent a decisive second conversion; both suffered long, hard, and humbly for love of Christ.

In solitary confinement, in the labor camps, Fr. Ciszek learned at last what Thérèse did in her Carmelite cell: "Each of us has no need to wonder about what God's will must be for us; his will for us is clearly revealed in every situation of every day."

MICHELANGELO

**Michelangelo di Lodovico Buonarroti Simoni
(1475-1564),** Italian sculptor, painter, and architect, is
widely acknowledged as one of the greatest artistic geniuses
of all time.

Born to a working class family, from the age of six he
displayed an interest in and talent for sculpting. As
a boy of thirteen, he caught the eye of Lorenzo de' Medici,
de facto ruler of the Florentine Republic. Lorenzo moved
Michelangelo into the household, where he lived for five
years. His exposure to the high-society worlds of art, politics,
and religion would be a major influence. He would also
struggle all his life for independence.

In 1492, Lorenzo died and, in the ensuing political upheaval,
Michelangelo fled Florence. He was enticed back in 1501
and, partly out of a desire to best his rival, Leonardo da
Vinci, obsessively applied himself to the thirteen-foot block
of Carrara marble that the world now knows as "David." For

two and a half years, he stinted on food, sleep, and human company. Legend has it that in his passion for work, he even forgot—or refused—to take off his boots at night.

His personal habits were rough, his living conditions squalid. *Bizzarro e fantastico*, the Italians called him: a man apart. "However rich I may have been, I have always lived like a poor man," he once told his apprentice. A mass of contradictions, he could be both self-sacrificing and petty, imperious and humble, obstinate and loyal. One thing is certain: he never married nor had children, devoting himself unreservedly to his work.

The highlights of his career are well-known: David, the Pietà, the Sistine Chapel Ceiling (Michelangelo knew nothing of fresco painting when the 3200-square foot work was commissioned by Pope Julius II), "The Last Judgment," the dome of St. Peter's Basilica, The Medici Chapel. He was astonishingly prolific, with sculptures, paintings, drawings, architectural works, poems, and even cartoons to his credit.

At the age of 73, he began work on the masterpiece that is now known as "The Deposition" (also sometimes called The Florentine Pietà). For ten years, while he completed commissioned architectural and painting projects, he chiseled away at his own creation, writing to his friend Vasari, "No project arises in my brain which hath not the figure of death graven upon it."

The sculpture depicts the Virgin Mary and Mary Magdalene waiting at the foot of the cross for Christ to be lowered into their arms by the aged Nicodemus—whose tender, tormented face Michelangelo modeled after himself. Out of frustration, possibly with the "imperfection" of his own work, Michelangelo later smashed the left arm and leg of Jesus.

Christ, of all people, would have sympathized. In his old age, Michelangelo was still trying to plumb the secrets of a block of white marble. Still reaching for perfection. Still straining—like Adam with his finger stretched across the ceiling of the Sistine Chapel—to touch the hand of God.

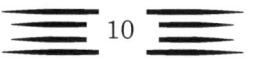

**SERVANT OF GOD
MARTHE ROBIN**

Marthe Robin (1902-1981), French mystic, stigmatic, and "victim soul," founded the Foyer de Charité, an organization whose mission is the giving of spiritual retreats with an emphasis on families.

As a youth, Robin was stricken with a mysterious illness. A few years later, she became completely paralyzed. From 1928 until her death over 50 years later, she was bedridden. She also ceased at that time to sleep or, with the exception of the Eucharist, to eat.

In 1929, she lost the use of her hands.

For most people, that would provide sufficient solidarity with the suffering of Christ. Not for Marthe. She then prayed to be—and was—blinded.

There was still more. In September, 1930, Christ came to her in a vision, she claimed, asking, "Do you want to be like Me?"

Naturally the answer was yes.

Every week thereafter, until the end of her life, each Thursday through Sunday, Robin re-experienced the Passion: the agony, the ecstasy, the hemorrhaging wounds.

We know, because people came and watched.

A skeptic might regard the dimly-lit room, the grainy photos of the blood-stained brow, the frilled bedcap and ask—to what end? An unkind person might be tempted to think that the real saints were the people who, for upwards of five decades, waited on her.

The trouble with oddities—and a person who doesn't sleep, move, or eat, other than the Eucharist for fifty years is an oddity—is that they inevitably draw more attention to themselves than to Christ. Robin had a steady stream of visitors. One hopes she constantly reminded them that the miracle was not her, but a God who creates human beings with the ability to eat and sleep in the first place.

Still, there are many rooms in our Father's mansion. By all accounts, Robin was cheerful, kind, and funny. Perhaps her real Crucifixion lay not in the fact that she couldn't eat or sleep, but that such a bizarre condition (or at least claim) unavoidably detracts from what well may have been her more hidden sanctity.

From her bed, Robin comforted, counseled and consoled thousands. She started a Christian school for girls. She founded the Foyers de Charité (Houses of Charity), retreat centers run by consecrated laypeople of which there are now at least 75 in 41 countries.

I feel about Marthe Robin a little like I feel about the occasional panhandler who appears to be completely normal: well-fed, well-groomed, well-dressed. That a rich person would stand on a street corner and beg is emblematic of a poverty that may be infinitely stranger, and more mysterious, than a mere lack of funds. Just so, any follower of Christ who lies in a bed for fifty years, receives visitors, and tries to lend a helping hand, for any reason, has to be some kind of saint.

Beethoven, deaf in the last years of his life, said, "In heaven, I shall hear." Let's hope that, in heaven, Marthe Robin can dance.

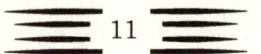

BROTHER LAWRENCE
OF THE RESURRECTION

Brother Lawrence of the Resurrection (c. 1614-1691), consecrated lay brother at a Discalced Carmelite monastery in Paris, is best known as the author of *The Practice of the Presence of God*.

Born Nicholas Herman in French Lorraine, Lawrence did poorly in school and worked briefly as a soldier and a valet, describing himself as "a great awkward fellow who broke everything." His conversion took place in the winter of his 18th year. Regarding a leafless tree he knew would burst into fruit at spring, he felt a deep and permanent sense of God, and ever after determined "to walk as in His presence."

He entered the monastery in 1666 and from that point forward was known as Brother Lawrence. Though he welcomed the prospect of being made "to smart" for his clumsiness, instead he was assigned to the kitchen and found that "God has disappointed him, he having met with nothing but satisfaction in that state."

Cleaning pots and scrubbing floors, Brother Lawrence grew quietly resplendent in love. We should continually converse with God, he learned, and refrain from concerning ourselves with anything other than carrying out His will. For one four-year period he became obsessed with the notion that he deserved to be, and would be, damned. Eventually he chalked up his tortured thoughts to a lack of faith, came to realize that God's abundance overcomes even our worst failings and sins, and from that day forward until he died in his late 70s, experienced perfect interior freedom and joy.

His spirituality has come down through his letters and jotted-down notes of conversations. Father Joseph de Beaufort compiled and first published the writings shortly after Brother Lawrence's death. Now known as *The Practice of the Presence of God*, the book is a small gem of a spiritual classic.

Whether Brother Lawrence was turning a frying cake, picking up a straw from the ground, or washing dishes, he "resolved to make the love of God the end of all his actions." He wrote:

"Lord of all pots and pans and things...
Make me a saint by getting meals
And washing up the plates!"

Brother Lawrence reminds us that in our day, God is also Lord of being stuck in commuter traffic, answering e-mails, and shopping for office supplies. Instead of fighting against our daily chores, whatever our station, Brother Lawrence invites us to lose ourselves in Christ: "Men invent means and methods of coming at God's love, they learn rules and set up devices to remind them of that love...Is it not quicker and easier just to do our common business wholly for the love of him?"

We sometimes erroneously think that the contemplative life can take place only in silence and solitude. These words of Brother Lawrence are as relevant to our busy, distracted times as they were almost 400 years ago:

"The time of business does not with me differ from the time of prayer, and in the noise and clatter of my kitchen, while several persons are at the same time calling for different things, I possess God in as great tranquility as if I were upon my knees at the Blessed Sacrament."

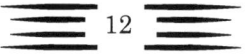

12

SERVANT OF GOD
FATHER LUKAS ETLIN

Fr. Lukas Etlin (1864-1927), artist, writer, and champion of nuns, seminarians and the dispossessed, was a monk at Conception Abbey in Conception, Missouri.

Born Alfred Etlin in the Swiss Alps, he made his way to the Benedictine abbey in Conception; professed as a monk in 1887, thereby entering consecrated life; and was ordained a priest in 1891.

His contributions were many. He was a talented artist: As the Abbey's website notes: "Between 1893 and 1897, several monks of Conception, most notable Lukas Etlin (d. 1927), Hildebrand Roseler (d. 1923), and Ildephonse Kuhn (d. 1921), the latter two of whom had studied art at Beuron [Germany], redecorated the walls and ceiling of the Abbey church primarily in the Beuronese manner, retaining elements of the original Victorian stenciling... Conception's was the first church in the United States so decorated. The apse painting of the Immaculate Conception is an original work by Lukas Etlin."

He was assigned as chaplain to the Benedictine Sisters of Perpetual Adoration in the adjacent town of Clyde. Fr. Etlin walked the two miles each way to celebrate Mass (he would eventually move to the convent). An ardent devotee of the liturgy and the Divine Office, he taught the sisters Gregorian chant, gave them spiritual direction, designed their Adoration Chapel, and set them on the road to their apostolate of altar bread work. Today the sisters bill themselves as "the largest religious producer of altar breads in the United States and the producer of the only low gluten altar bread approved by the Vatican."

As overseer of the nearby Our Lady of Victory Orphanage, he encouraged the local children to send care packages to the needy overseas. Though "Tabernacle and Purgatory" (now "Spirit & Life"), the magazine he published from the convent starting in 1905, he raised over two million dollars in relief funds that were disbursed across Europe and China to aid famine victims after the WWI Armistice.

The seminarian scholarship program spearheaded by Fr. Etlin by one count "helped 2800 men become priests … including 3 cardinals, 5 archbishops, 11 bishops, 9 auxiliary bishops and 14 abbots."

In the long pamphlet he wrote called "The Holy Eucharist: Our All", Fr. Etlin observed, "Without the Holy Eucharist, earth would seem to us empty, the temple of God desolate, the soul cold, the heart isolated. Oh God, this earth is a vale of tears where I weep and sigh! Here I cannot remain alone—alone with people who are careless and indifferent to my suffering; I have need of Thee!"

The pamphlet concludes with this prayer:

"[A]nnihilate in me all guilty, sensual and undue love for creatures; kindle in my heart the pure flame of Thy love, so that I may love nothing but Thee or in Thee, until being entirely consumed by holy love of Thee"...

On the morning of December 16, 1927, Fr. Etlin offered Mass at the convent in Clyde, then taught a class at St. Joseph's Academy, telling the girls, "We must at all times be ready to die."

Later that day he was the victim of a fatal car crash. He left this world clutching his rosary.

 13

SÉRAPHINE LOUIS DE SENLIS

Séraphine Louis, better known as **Séraphine de Senlis (1864-1942)**, French "outsider artist," worked as a convent maid before being "discovered" and died in an insane asylum.

Séraphine was born to a peasant family in the village of Arsy in northern France. She was orphaned by the age of 6. Her eldest sister cared for her during one period. She supported herself for a time as a shepherdess.

By 1881, when she was 17, she was engaged as a domestic worker at the Sisters of Providence convent in Clermont, Oise.

From 1901 on, she worked as a charwoman for middle-class families in the nearby town of Senlis.

In 1912, German art collector Wilhelm Uhde was visiting Senlis when he chanced to see a still-life of apples at the home of his host and learned that the artist was the man's housecleaner, Séraphine.

There were many more such paintings, it turned out, of exuberant flowers, fruits and trees—"The Lord's Garden," Séraphine summed up this celestial paradise. A fervent Catholic, she was inspired by the fields and woods through which since childhood she had loved to walk. She made her own paints from a secret recipe that may have included oil from the tapers burned in church, moss, clay, and blood.

Uhde was also a champion of Rousseau, Picasso and Braque. Of Séraphine, he observed: "An extraordinary passion, a sacred fervor, a medieval ardor."

"What can I tell you, Sir?" she remarked to Uhde. "I paint as I pray. There's no difference. I always say that I do all this for the Virgin Mary. I paint above all at night when the town is asleep. My still lifes are like gifts for the Good Lord and the Holy Mother. Necklaces of pearls and precious stones that I thread so they'll be pleased with me. So I'll go to Paradise."

Uhde supplied Séraphine with painting materials, encouraged and supported her in every way, and saw to it that she was included among the "naïve artists," as such unschooled painters were called, who flourished between the two World Wars.

Uhde was forced to flee France at the outbreak of WWI. When he returned in 1927, he assumed Séraphine had died, and was amazed instead to find her work mounted in a local exhibit.

Always an eccentric, however, she had become ever more

prone to visions and states of near-ecstasy. Poverty and ill-treatment she could deal with. It was perhaps even a small measure of success that sent her over the edge.

In 1932, Séraphine was admitted to the lunatic asylum at Clermont. The diagnosis was chronic psychosis. By all accounts, she never painted again.

She died in 1934 (some accounts say 1942), penniless and alone, and was buried in a common grave.

Her paintings are today exhibited in the Musée d'art de Senlis, the Musée d'art naïf in Nice, and the Musée d'Art moderne Lille Métropole in Villeneuve-d'Ascq.

And in heaven she must surely sit at the Virgin's knee: gazing out over her beloved fields, still exuberantly praising; still painting her numinous and mysterious flowers.

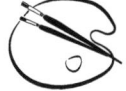

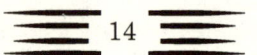

BLESSED FRANZ JÄGERSTÄTTER

Franz Jägerstätter (1907-1943), Austrian peasant, conscientious objector, husband, and father of three, refused to fight for the Nazis and died by the guillotine.

Annemarie S. Kidder tells the story in *Ultimate Price: Testimonies of Christians Who Resisted the Third Reich.* After fathering a child out of wedlock in 1933, Jägerstätter fell in love with and married Franziska Schwaninger, a devout Catholic, the next year. They honeymooned as Easter pilgrims in Rome.

He fathered three more children, became a third-order Franciscan, and happily ran the family farm. Though his formal education had ended in seventh grade, Jägerstätter read widely, pondered deeply, and prayed constantly— especially about the social and political climate of his country at that time in light of the Gospels.

In 1938, Jägerstätter cast the only vote in his village against joining the Third Reich. He underwent military training from 1940-41, but the experience only sharpened his resolve to resist serving under Hitler. To his wife he wrote: "Christ said that whoever wants to be my disciple must take up his cross and follow me."

In notebooks he kept from 1941-43, he remarked upon, but did not blame, the Catholic priests and bishops who had chosen to go along with the Nazis and counseled their parishioners to do the same. He dreamed one night of a train that was going to hell. He asked himself: "What must people of other beliefs think about us and about our Christian belief when we value it so little?"

On March 2, 1943, he refused to take the oath of combat for the Nazis. He was arrested and imprisoned for two months at Linz, then transferred to Berlin's Tegel Penitentiary.

The letters and essays he wrote in his last weeks remind us that authentic followers of Christ do not rail, accuse and hate. They extend mercy. Regardless of public opinion, in and out of the Church, they remain fiercely faithful to the Gospels—even at the cost of their own lives. They can say, even while in prison, "Let us love one another and readily forgive each other. Most people embitter their lives by their lack of reconciliation."

To criticisms leveled by fellow Catholics that he was

neglecting his moral duty as a husband and father, Jägerstätter rejoined: "Is someone permitted to lie in taking an oath just because he has a wife and children? Did not Christ himself say that whoever loves a wife, mother and children more than me is not worthy of me?"

From his cell, he celebrated the "beautiful May devotions" to Mary with a dried violet sent by his daughter Rosalia.

Two days after being condemned to death, he wrote in a letter to his wife, mother, father-in-law, and children: "It is a joy to be able to suffer for Jesus and our friends." He did not mention the death sentence.

His last wish, conveyed by a letter to his wife dated August 9, 1943, was to celebrate the feast of Mary's Assumption in heaven.

He was beheaded that afternoon at 4 o'clock as an "enemy of the state."

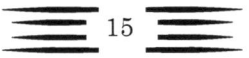

BLESSED
BARTOLO LONGO

Bartolo Longo (1841-1926), former Satanist priest, returned to the Catholic faith, became a third order Dominican, and devoted his life to the Rosary and the Virgin Mary.

Born to a devout Catholic Italian family in 1841, as a child Bartolo frequently prayed the rosary with his parents and siblings. But his mother died when he was 10 and, while at college in Naples, he fell in with members of an occult group, lapsed completely from the faith, and began engaging in séances, fortune-telling and orgies.

He even went so far as to be ordained a Satanic priest. He performed black masses and, at every turn, publicly ridiculed Catholicism. But he also fell into nervous exhaustion, depression, and melancholia.

One day he heard the voice of his deceased father, entreating: "Return to God! Return to God!" He turned to an old friend from his hometown, Professor Vincenzo Pepe, for spiritual guidance. Shocked at Bartolo's decrepit appearance, the professor asked: "Do you want to die in an insane asylum, and then be damned forever?"

The question brought Bartolo to his senses. Under Professor Pepe's guidance, he forswore Satan. Fr. Alberto Radente, a Dominican priest, heard his Confession. Bartolo undertook to redeem his life.

At the age of 30, on the Feast of the Assumption, he became a Third Order Lay Dominican. He took the name Brother Rosario, after Mary and his renewed devotion to the Rosary.

He restored a church in Pompeii, installing a thrift-store painting of the Blessed Virgin. Miracles occurred. Pilgrims flocked to the site. In a treatise entitled "The History of the Shrine of Pompeii" Bartolo cast his work as a corrective to the eruption of Mt. Vesuvius in 79 AD, writing:

"Next to a land of dead appeared, quite suddenly, a land of resurrection and life: next to a shattered amphitheatre soiled with blood, there is a living Temple of faith and love, a sacred Temple to the Virgin Mary."

"What is my vocation? To write about Mary, to have Mary praised, to have Mary loved."

In 1885, Longo entered into a chaste marriage with Countess Mariana di Fusco, a wealthy widow who shared his passion for charitable works.

He tirelessly supported orphans and the poor, attended Confession twice weekly, and in his later years, gave all his property to the Holy See.

One inhabitant of Pompeii observed, "I often saw him with his arms outstretched and his eyes fixed on heaven or on the image of Our Lady, or even with his eyes half-closed, totally enraptured without being aware of those around or near him."

His last words were reputed to have been: "My only desire is to see Mary, who has saved me and who will save me from the clutches of Satan."

Blessed Bartolo reminds us of three things. One: the Church has never claimed to be a bastion of mental health. Two: no-one is beyond redemption. And three: the more impure we have been, the more we need Mary.

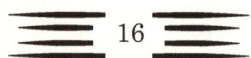 16

**SERVANT OF GOD
ADELE DIRSYTÉ**

Adele Dirsyté (1919-1955), tortured and martyred in Communist Russia, wrote the prayer book *Mary, Save Us* while imprisoned in Siberia.

Born in Lithuania to parents who were farmers, Adele was the youngest of six children. At college she majored in philosophy, then worked for various youth organizations. Among them was Caritas, which served widows and orphans. She taught German at a girls' school, leading her students in prayer and retreats.

The Soviet occupation of Lithuania began in 1940. In June 1941, Germany attacked the USSR and soon occupied the Baltic territories. During the Nazi occupation, Adele lived with a woman who was harboring a Jewish girl.

By 1944, the Soviet army had reoccupied the capital city of Vilnius. Adele began participating in a resistance movement that was organizing for Lithuanian independence.

In 1946, she was arrested for hiding a woman who had escaped from the Soviets. She was brought before a tribunal, and sentenced for "counterrevolutionary activities" to ten years in a concentration camp.

Imprisoned for a year in Vilnius, she was then transferred to what would be the first of a series of forced labor camps. She and her fellow inmates hacked trees, moved rocks, and built railways, They also endured bitter cold, poor sanitary conditions, and starvation rations.

Adele was known for her kindness, faith, and steadfast efforts to console and comfort her fellow prisoners. At Magadan concentration camp, she managed to produce a small prayer book, hand-sewn with cloth covers. Other inmates were encouraged to add their own hand-written prayers as the book made the rounds of the barracks. Originally called *Prayer Book for Girls Exiled in Siberia*, the little volume eventually found its way to the West and is now known as *Mary, Save Us*.

One day a priest inmate from the adjacent men's camp arranged for the Eucharist to be brought over and distributed among the Lithuanian women. The guards noticed and, over the coming months, Adele was taken repeatedly to a cold underground cell and beaten. All her teeth were knocked out. Her fellow inmates realized she had been marked for "slow extermination."

In the fall of 1953 she was held in the punishment cell for a week, then transferred to an unknown location for the winter. She returned to Magadan partially incoherent, with half of her hair torn out, and was moved to a ward for the mentally ill. Here she refused food, saying "You who work must eat." She died on September 26, 1955. The cause for her beatification was opened on January 14, 2000.

One detail, from her time before prison, haunts. A former student remarked "She was modest and very quiet... Her lessons were a bit boring."

Her lessons were a bit boring. How sharply we are reminded that the person marked out by Christ to share his crown is often outwardly ordinary and without special talents.

Her lessons were a bit boring. And within Servant of God Adele Dirsyté burned the heart of a martyr, a queen, a saint.

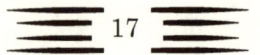

**SERVANT OF GOD
FATHER STANLEY ROTHER**

Fr. Stanley Rother (1935-1981), missionary to Guatemala during a brutal civil war, refused to leave his parishioners and was murdered by a paramilitary death squad.

As a boy, Stanley tilled the fields of his father's farm in Okarche, Oklahoma. Scholarship was not his forté. He flunked a semester at the seminary, felled by Latin.

Ordained a priest in 1963, he served in several Oklahoma parishes before being assigned to Guatemala. In 1968, he drove 2000 miles by car to arrive at his missionary post in the village of Santiago Atitlán. Many of his parishioners were Tzutujil Indians, descendants of the Mayans. Poverty and disease were endemic. Up to half of the village children died of malnutrition before the age of six.

He insisted upon working beside the people he served, tilling the fields, digging wells, and driving a tractor. He translated the New Testament into the native language, visited the peasants in their homes, and celebrated up to five Masses each Sunday.

"He didn't want to change their culture," later remarked his sister Marita, a nun. "Rather than take away, he was trying to integrate [Catholicism]."

In the 1970's, Guatemala was torn by civil war, with the right-wing, U.S.-backed government pitted against left-wing guerillas who dared to speak of the plight of the poor. Though Fr. Rother refrained from preaching rebellion, the government suspected the Church of colluding with the guerillas and killed several priests. Community members, including a former deacon, were "disappeared." Others were tortured or murdered.

By 1981, Fr. Rother's name was on the hit list of a right-wing death squad. Family and friends begged him to leave Guatemala. Reluctantly, he moved for several weeks through a series of safe houses, then returned to Oklahoma.

But away from his flock, Fr. Rother could not be at rest. He sat staring listlessly out the window. It was as if he knew his destiny, and neither wanted, nor sought, to avoid it.

He told Archbishop Charles Salatka of the Oklahoma City Archdiocese, "My people need me, I can't stay away from them any longer." The Archbishop granted permission to return.

By that, time, Fr. Rother was the only one left from the staff of eleven that had greeted him upon his initial arrival. He had served the people of Guatemala for thirteen years.

Mere months later, he was shot to death in his rectory by three paramilitary assassins . The news spread throughout the region like wildfire. By dawn, thousands of Tzutujil stood vigil around the church.

"It was as if they'd lost their God," noted Raymond Bailey, a U.S. Embassy staff member who arrived that morning from Guatemala City. "It was a sight I'll remember the rest of my life."

In the end, the shepherd who would not leave his flock came home. His body, clad in the red vestments of a martyr, was laid to rest at the Holy Trinity Cemetery in Okarche.

But at the behest of the villagers whom he loved and served, Fr. Rother left his heart—literally—in Guatemala. The peasants buried it beneath the altar of the Santiago Atitlán church.

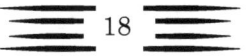

JAN TYRANOWSKI

Jan Tyranowski (1900-1947), Catholic layman and student of Discalced Carmelite spirituality, served a crucial role as spiritual advisor to the young Karol Wojtyla, who later became Pope John Paul II.

An eccentric figure with white blond hair and a distinctive, high-pitched voice, Tyranowski lived with his mother and several cats across the street from the Wojtylas in Poland. He made his way as a tailor, remained voluntarily celibate, and cultivated an intense prayer life, often aggressively trying to recruit the young people of the neighborhood to participate in his "Living Rosary."

In February, 1940, Wojtyla was 20. Tyranowski was 40. The two met at a meeting in a local parish hall. Immediately the future Pope was drawn by Tyranowski's mystical fervor.

Well-meaning friends, including the future priest Mieczyslaw Malinski tried to warn off the young Wojtyla, insinuating that Tyranowski had spent time in mental institutions and psychiatric wards. But where others saw pathology, the man who would become Pope John Paul II saw passion.

"Tyranowski has gone through a major life-changing conversion," Wojtyla observed. "Look at what is inside him, not his outward experience. Yes, he speaks in a slightly odd, affected manner, but look beyond that. He is a man who lives truly close to God."

A year after they met, Wojtyla's father died. Shattered by the blow, young Karol spent more and more time with Tyranowski—whose spiritual guidance was crucial. The two endlessly discussed Scripture as well as the mystical writers Teresa of Avila and St. John of the Cross.

Biographer Tad Szulc tells the story of the friendship more fully in *Pope John Paul II*. Szulc emphasizes Tyranowski's strangeness, including his tendency to speak in clerical platitudes and to use archaic language that at first grated on Wojtyla. Tyranowski could be so pushy and aggressive that Wojtyla's friend Malinski at first thought the tailor might be a Gestapo agent.

But after Tyranowski's death, Wojtyla penned a tribute styling him "an apostle" and "someone really saintly." His gift was to touch upon and draw out the depths in men's souls: "The plenitude of inner life," as he called it.

"I must decrease; He must increase," observed John the Baptist, a truth Tyranowski, bending over his needle and thread, must have known well. A lifelong loner, he would have heard and felt deeply the taunts of the neighborhood children. An eccentric with a profound mystical bent, he would have been very much aware of his existential exile. A reader of men's souls, he seemed to have sensed that his friend, the future Pope, was destined for greatness.

His response was gladly to take last place himself.

The economy of the world rewards numbers, efficiency, flash. God's economy is pearl buried in a field, a seed sowed in secret, the servant who lays down his life so that a friend's tree might bear fruit.

As Pope John Paul II noted: "Tyranowski was truly one of those unknown saints, hidden among others like a marvelous light at the bottom of life at a depth where night usually reigns."

19

CHRISTINA OF MARKYATE

Christina of Markyate was born circa **1095-1100** in East Anglia to wealthy merchant parents. Her home town of Huntingdon had a strong charism for the Virgin Mary. As a child, she visited the Benedictine Abbey of St. Albans and became attracted by the monastic way of life.

Having taken a vow of virginity, she spurned the advances of Ranulf Flambard, bishop of Durham. With the collusion of her parents, the bishop forced her into an arranged marriage with a man named Beorhtred: a union Christina steadfastly refused to consummate.

Instead, she fled close to St. Albans so as to escape being found out by her husband and lived for three years as a female recluse. Next she went to Markyate and, under the protection of an elderly monk named Roger, lived in a tiny cell, suffering hunger, thirst, and cold.

Each day Roger let her out for an hour, took her to chapel,

and taught her the secrets of prayer. Rumors sprang up. But grounded securely in Christ, and the marriage of Christ and his Church, Roger and Christina were of great help to one another. In fact, one of Christina's great themes would be spiritual friendship—men and women who inspire, support, and encourage one another to grow in the love of Christ.

Beorhtred eventually released Christina from her vows. The marriage was dissolved, leaving her free to choose where to live out her religious vocation. Though the 12th-century monastic Renaissance in Europe gave her many opportunities, she elected to return to Markyate, which Roger had left to her at his death circa 1121.

She made her formal profession as a consecrated nun in 1130 or 1131. A community grew up around her, which in 1145 was declared a priory. By that time, Roger had died. Christina formed a friendship with Geoffrey, abbot of St. Albans, who provided much-needed financial and spiritual support.

Geoffrey died in 1146. We do not know when Christina died or where she is buried. No movement was made to canonize her after her death, but the community at Markyate survived and flourished until Henry VIII dissolved it. We know of her story and spirituality through a manuscript—*The Life of Christina of Markyate*—believed to have been written by a St. Albans monk with whom she was personally acquainted.

The lengths to which she went to preserve her virginity against physical and emotional threats, family exile, and pressure from the Church were extraordinary. At one point, after the death of Roger, she encountered a religious man who turned out to be a false friend and to whom she was violently attracted. She "vehemently resisted the desires of her own flesh" by "long fasting, little food and only raw herbs at that, a ration of drink, sleepless nights, and harsh scourgings." She also had visions.

Her parents had wanted to marry her off to a rich husband, and for years accused her of holding out for someone even wealthier than Beorhtred.

"A more wealthy one certainly," she replied, "for who is richer than Christ?"

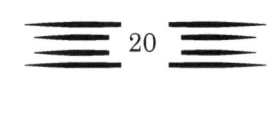

SIR ALEC GUINNESS

Sir Alec Guinness (1914-2000), renowned British actor, converted to Catholicism after playing a priest in the 1954 film *The Detective* aka *Father Brown*.

Perhaps best known for his role as the bearded sage Obi-Wan Kenobi in the Star Wars films, Guinness was born into a broken family. His mother Agnes Cuffe was unmarried. He never knew his father. Abused by a brutal stepfather, as an adolescent Guinness discovered the solace of the theater. Confirmed into the Anglican church at 16, as a youth he dabbled in various religions while secretly considering himself an atheist.

Religion, he believed, was "so much rubbish, a wicked scheme of the Establishment to keep the working man in his place."

Acclaimed for his role of Hamlet on the London stage, he went on to launch what would prove to be an equally illustrious film career: *Oliver Twist* (1948), *Kind Hearts and Coronets* (1949), *The Man in the White Suit* (1951).

In 1954, he was cast as the lead in *The Detective*, a film based on the character of G.K. Chesterton's crime-solving priest, Fr. Brown. On location in France, he was walking down the street one evening, still clad in his stage vestments, when a local child mistook him for a real priest, trustingly took Guinness's hand, and began accompanying him down the street.

In *Blessings in Disguise*, Volume 1 of his autobiography, he wrote of the incident:

> *Continuing my walk I reflected that a Church which could inspire such confidence in a child, making its priests, even when unknown, so easily approachable could not be as scheming or as creepy as so often made out. I began to shake off my long-taught, long-absorbed prejudices.*

Just before filming began, the actor's son Matthew, 11, had contracted polio. Guinness began ducking into "a rather tawdry little" local Catholic church to pray. He made a bargain with God: if Matthew were healed, he wouldn't object should the boy ever express a desire to convert to Catholicism.

Matthew did recover, and Guinness and his wife subsequently enrolled him in a Jesuit school. Meanwhile, Guinness himself continued to seek God, and was confirmed as a Catholic in 1956. Merula followed the next year. Matthew came into the Church at the age of 15.

"There had been no emotional upheaval," Guinness wrote, "no great insight, certainly no proper grasp of theological issues; just a sense of history and the fittingness of things."

He was knighted by Queen Elizabeth II in 1959 for services to the arts.

A frequent communicant for the remaining decades of his life, he died of liver cancer on August 5, 2000. Merula passed away two months later. The two had been married 60 years.

Watching Guinness now, it's lovely to contemplate the source from which his devotion to family and art sprang. He once described walking a London street when, with joy in his heart, he began running. "I ran until I reached the little Catholic church there ... which I had never entered before; I knelt; caught my breath, and for ten minutes was lost to the world."

CARLO CARRETTO

Carlo Carretto (1910-1988), Italian writer, mystic, and member of the Little Brothers of Jesus, modeled himself upon desert contemplative Charles de Foucauld.

Born and raised in northern Italy, as a youth Carretto joined the lay movement Catholic Action. For twenty years he worked to spread the religious and social justice message of the Gospels in and around fascist Italy.

In 1954, he felt the desert call and set out for the Sahara. In El Abiodh, a remote Algerian outpost, he entered the novitiate of the Little Brothers of Jesus, a community of desert contemplatives based on the spirituality of St. Francis of Assisi that had been founded by de Foucauld in the 1930s. Monastic austerity and silent adoration were to be combined with a life of humble labor, friendship, and solidarity with one's immediate neighbors.

A decisive moment—a "cut"—occurred when Carretto burned

the address book containing the contact information for thousands of his friends back in Italy. He stayed for ten years as a hermit: translating the Bible into Bedouin, sitting for hours before the Blessed Sacrament in prayer.

At last he left the Sahara, returned to his hometown and went to visit his beloved mother who, for more than thirty years, had been living an active life, crowded with family, social, and parish responsibilities. Perhaps the surest sign of Carretto's sanctity is this: He recognized that for all his time in the desert, his mother was at least the contemplative that he was.

The missives he had sent back were published as *Letters From the Desert*, his first book, in 1964 in Italy. A bestseller, the book was translated and published in English in 1972.

In it, he observed:

> *"Jesus is the 'Holy One of God.' But the Holy One of God realized his sanctity not in extraordinary life, but one impregnated with ordinary things: work, family and social life, obscure human activities, simple things shared by all men. The perfection of God is cast in a material which men almost despise, which they don't consider worth searching for because of its simplicity, its lack of interest, because it is common to all men."*

Soon after returning to Italy, Carretto was asked to oversee a group of hermitages the Little Brothers had established near Assisi. He stayed for the rest of his life, welcoming the flocks of pilgrims who came to learn about prayer and reflection, and writing a dozen or so more books.

In *I, Francis*, Carretto "takes on" the voice of his spiritual mentor.

On the subject of politics, he observed: "Try being governed by those who can still look at the stars at night, or spend an hour watching a beetle under a dry leaf in the forest, or dream over a glow-worm in a field of May wheat."

On poverty: "At the vespers of your life you will be judged by your love, not by your poverty... Never forget, God is love. Poverty is but his garment."

Prayer is useless, Carretto realized, unless it helps us to grow in charity. He died in the hills of Umbria, after a long illness, at the age of 78.

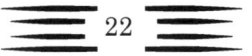 22

CATHERINE
DE HUECK DOHERTY

Catherine de Hueck Doherty (1896-1985), Russian émigré, lover of the poor, and contemplative, founded Madonna House, a haven for the homeless and a training center for the lay apostolate in Canada.

Doherty came from a long line of Russian hermit-mystics who wandered the countryside with the Jesus prayer— "Lord Jesus Christ, Son of the Living God, have mercy on me, a sinner"—in their hearts. She married American journalist Eddie Doherty, and was herself a prolific writer.

In *Strannik*, a Russian word meaning "pilgrim," she observed that while all are called to pilgrimage, few can or will go. Pilgrimage doesn't necessarily involve traveling, or traveling into the country. The journey is to our own hearts, and can thus take place in the *poustinia* (a sparse hut or room) of our apartments, or by walking through the streets of a city. Wherever we go, we go with bare feet—in spiritual poverty— and because we end up walking into the fragmented stones and sharp rocks of other people's hearts, our feet get bloody.

We're chaste, we're obedient, we fast and, like Christ, we're constantly called to move on to another place. We can't be tempted by spiritual riches and gifts, and always we make ourselves available to the people in our lives and those we meet. Sensing that we're walking the spiritual path, these people ask us about God, and after a while we notice them changing a bit around us.

This often happens in the most ordinary, even dreary, circumstances. Doherty tells the story of working as a salesclerk in a department store. When the personnel manager learned that she was making the highest commissions, he called her in to ask the secret of her success.

> "I said, 'Well, nothing special happens. I like selling, but that's not the point. The point is that I made a contract with your company to be on the job eight hours a day. There is my lunch hour, and there are moments when I have to depart from the floor—nature calls! But I consider all the rest of it is yours. I do not consider it is a time to talk to the other salesclerks or to go and powder my nose again and again. That's not my idea. I consider a contract is a moral affair, the more so because I made it also with God.'"

> "I had a moral obligation to spend eight hours a day selling," she continued. "If I didn't want to sell, I could

quit, but I couldn't fritter away the time, for this would be wrong. The pilgrim knows this as he walks that road of moral obligation which is, after all, the duty of the moment. My duty was selling."

Voluntarily poor, she did not use her convictions to justify stealing from her employer. Her love for the poor extended, as our love must, to the rich, the corporate, the profiteers.

"A pilgrim preaches the gospel," she observed, "but in order to preach it he has to live it day by day, hour by hour, minute by minute. For what is he really about, that pilgrim of mine? He is preaching the gospel with his life and so his pilgrimage has to reflect his life."

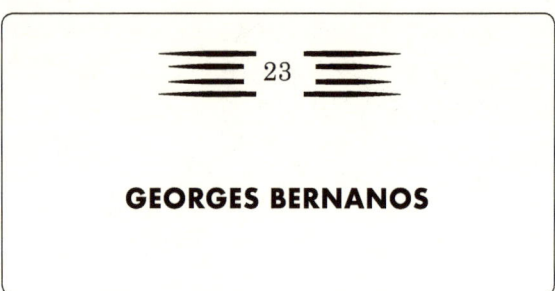

GEORGES BERNANOS

Georges Bernanos (1888-1948), award winning French writer, authored the iconic novel *Diary of a Country Priest*.

Born in Paris to a devout Roman Catholic family of craftsmen, as a youth Bernanos joined the conservative Action Française movement. After serving as a soldier in WWI, however, he broke with the movement. At the time France was deeply divided: conservative monarchists, liberal republicans, anti-Catholic agnostics. Bernanos began noticing the poor and disenfranchised and wondering why the Church didn't do more for them.

He married in 1917. He and his wife would go on to have six children.

Bernanos was a wanderer, perpetually short of money and fiercely contemptuous of literary salon society. In 1932, he moved with his family to Majorca where he wrote what would be his masterpiece: *Diary of a Country Priest*.

The protagonist, a sickly young priest, has a heart on fire for Christ, parishioners who are "bored stiff," and stomach cancer. Unable to keep down more than bread and a glass of wine, he's accused by the townsfolk of being drunkard. When he tries to help a young girl, she jeeringly tries to seduce him. The Countess, whose soul he desperately tries to save, rages against God for taking her infant son.

Small wonder the priest notes: "How glibly we talk about 'family-life,' as we do also of 'my country.' We ought to say many prayers for families. Families frighten me. May God be merciful with them."

Published in 1936, the novel was both popularly and critically acclaimed, winning the coveted Grand Prix du roman de l'Académie française.

But Bernanos was increasingly disillusioned by the spiritual bankruptcy of European politics, and by the failure of his beloved Church to model the teachings of Christ. In 1938, he published *Les Grandes Cimetières Sous la Lune* (Great Cemeteries Under the Moon), decrying the terror that was being inflicted by Franco on innocent men, women and children in the name of Catholic nationalism.

That same year, he emigrated to South America with his family and settled in Brazil. Over the course of his career, he wrote essays, plays, and several more novels.

Courted by de Gaulle, Bernanos returned to France in 1945 but the homecoming was a disappointment. A loner till the end, Bernanos died near Paris at the age of 60.

In 1951, French director Robert Bresson released a film based on *Diary of a Country Priest. The Guardian* called the performance of Claude Laydu, in his debut role, one of the greatest in the history of film.

As for Bernanos, he could have been the protagonist of his most well-known book. Like his sickly young priest, he consented to open his veins for the flock he served, to remain faithful in a world hostile to religion, to live with results so meager he must have wondered whether they were results at all. To feel oneself an ineffective witness, to plow forward anyway: this is the lot of every follower of Christ.

The priest's dying words are "Grace is everywhere." But perhaps his very last word is this: "Hell is not to love any more."

24

GREGOR JOHANN MENDEL

Gregor Johann Mendel (1822-1884) scientist,
Augustinian friar and abbot, founded the modern science
of genetics.

Mendel was born in what was then Heinzendorf, Austria
(now part of the Czech Republic), and lived on the
family farm until age 11. He graduated in 1843 from the
Philosophical Institute of the University of Olmütz with high
marks in physics and math, in spite of suffering bouts of
extreme depression.

Also in 1843, Mendel joined the Augustinian order at the St.
Thomas Monastery in Brno. He took the name Gregor and
was ordained a priest in 1847.

After failing in his efforts to become a certified high school
teacher, in 1851 he was sent by the monastery to the
University of Vienna to continue studying the sciences. His

physics professor there was Christian Doppler, renowned for his articulation of the Doppler Effect.

He returned to the monastery in 1853. Dissatisfied with Darwin's theory of evolution, between1856 and 1863 Mendel embarked on a deeply fruitful period of plant experimentation. He discovered the principles of heredity through working in the monastery garden.

He chose peas because they were cheap, easily produced and came in many varieties. He cross-fertilized plants using seven opposite traits: height—a tall would be bred with a short, for example—pod shape and unripe color, seed shape and color, and flower position and color.

Two of his most notable discoveries were the "Law of Segregation" which, in layman's terms, established the existence of dominant and recessive traits that are randomly passed on from parents to offspring. The "Law of Independent Assortment" established that traits are passed from parents to offspring independently of other traits.

Together, these later became known as Mendel's Laws of Inheritance. He extrapolated that all living things were subject to them.

In 1865 he presented two lectures on his experiments to the Natural Science Society in Brno. Both papers were largely ignored and had little impact. He did little further promotion or publicizing of his work.

Mendel was also drawn to meteorology, astronomy, and bees, the latter which he'd begun keeping and studying as a child: "my dearest little animals," he called them. He became abbot at Brno in 1867. The burden of administrative duties largely foreclosed further experimentation with plants, a fact that by many accounts hung heavy on his heart.

One wonders if he ever discovered a dominant gene for the trait of obedience. Though disappointed by the seeming failure of his life's work, he reportedly told a friend: "My time will come."

He died at the age of 61, discouraged and in pain, and was buried in the monastery garden.

Only decades later, at the dawn of the 20th century, were his ground-breaking discoveries recognized. His findings and methods have been contested. Few dispute, however, that as he toiled obscurely away in the shadow of the monastery church, cross-fertilizing his beloved peas, Mendel paved the way for the science of modern genetics.

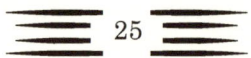 25

FLANNERY O'CONNOR

Flannery O'Connor (1925-1964), award-winning American novelist and short story writer, was an only child whose father died of lupus. As a young woman she studied at the prestigious Iowa Workshop. On the verge of a promising literary career, she contracted lupus herself and returned to the family dairy farm in Milledgeville, Georgia, to live out her remaining days with her mother.

A daily Mass-goer in the overwhelmingly evangelical South, O'Connor referred to herself as a "hillbilly Thomist" and often read a page or two from the *Summa Theologica* before going to bed. She never married.

Closely observing the people with whom she came in contact every day, she wrote stories about intellectual pride, the perils of secular humanism, and the violence of grace that, even today, have the power to shock.

In "Good Country People" Hulga, a would-be nihilist home from college, is seduced by a traveling Bible salesman who lures her to a hayloft, then steals her wooden leg.

In *Wise Blood*, backwoods preacher Hazel Motes blinds himself with quicklime.

"Jesus thrown everything off balance," notes The Misfit, the escaped convict in "A Good Man is Hard to Find." Then he shoots the entire family, including the grandmother.

"Can't you write things that would make a little more money?" O'Connor's mother Regina kept asking.

In the preface to O'Connor's collected letters, editor Sally Fitzgerald observed that it was from Jacques Maritain that O'Connor "first learned the conception of 'the habit of art,' habit in this instance being defined in the Scholastic mode, not as mere mechanical routine, but as an attitude or quality of mind, as essential to the real artist as talent."

O'Connor wrote every day, tended her beloved peacocks, entertained guests as her health allowed, and had a finely-honed sense of humor.

On making a living with writing: "There's no money in it and little consolation except that it looks good when you have to fill out a form...And a year later you will get a few letters from your friends saying they say your book for 33 cents on a remainder table."

Of her faith: "I am a Catholic not like someone else would be a Baptist or a Methodist, but like someone else would be an atheist."

Of vocation: "We are not judged by what we are basically. We are judged by how hard we use what we have been given. Success means nothing to the Lord…"

On examination of conscience: The 12-year old girl known only as "the child" in "A Temple of the Holy Ghost" prays: "Hep me not to be so mean. Hep me not to give [my mother] so much sass. Hep me not to talk like I do."

Swollen with cortisone, her joints crippled, devoid to the end of self-pity, O'Connor worked fiercely through the lupus that would kill her at the age of 39.

She left us with these words that could have been written in her own blood: "The Catholic writer, in so far as he has the mind of the Church, will feel life from the standpoint of the central Christian mystery; that it has, for all its horror, been found by God to be worth dying for."

OLIVIER MESSIAEN

Olivier Messiaen (1908-1992), French, composed "Quartet For the End of Time" while a German prisoner of war during WWII. The piece was first performed by Messiaen and fellow prisoners before an audience of 5000 guards and inmates.

Born in Avignon, as a child Messiaen asked for musical scores rather than toys for Christmas. In Catholicism, he found "the marvelous multiplied a hundredfold, a thousandfold."

He began composing at 7, taught himself piano, and entered the Paris Conservatoire at the age of 11. He visited Saint Chapelle that year and, "overwhelmed by the colors of the stained glass windows," began mentally transposing them into sound, an example of a perceptual phenomenon known as synaesthesia.

In 1932, he married the violinist and composer Claire Delbos.

Their son Pascal was born in 1937. Delbos later underwent an operation, lost her memory, and was institutionalized for the remainder of her life.

Drafted into the Army as a medic at the outbreak of WWII, Messiaen was captured by the Nazis in May, 1940, and imprisoned at Görlitz's Stalag VIII-A.

"Quartet for the End of Time" was based on the only four instruments available in the camp: violin, cello, clarinet and piano. A friendly German officer smuggled in manuscript paper and pencils and allowed Messiaen to work in the priests' block.

He went on after the war to a long and distinguished career. He developed such innovative techniques as limited transposition, additive rhythms, and chord coloration. He often incorporated birdsong into his compositions. His "Treatise on Rhythm, Color and Ornithology" (1949–1992) runs to eight volumes.

Messiaen died in Paris on April 27, 1992, leaving a prodigious body of work, much of it sacred. But "Quartet for the End of Time," based on Revelation 10:1-7, remains probably his most-performed composition.

Of its January 15, 1941, premiere, he wrote:

*"It took place in Görlitz, in Silesia, in a dreadful cold.
Stalag was buried in snow. We were 30,000 prisoners
(French for the most part, with a few Poles and Belgians).
The four musicians played on broken instruments: Etienne
Pasquier's cello had only 3 strings; the keys of my upright
piano remained lowered when depressed... It's on this
piano, with my three fellow musicians, dressed in the
oddest way — I myself wearing a bottle-green suit of a
Czech soldier — completely tattered, and wooden clogs
large enough for the blood to circulate despite the snow
underfoot... that I played...before an audience of 5,000
people.* The most diverse classes of society were
mingled: farmers, factory workers, intellectuals,
professional servicemen, doctors, priests.
Never before have I been listened to with such
attention and understanding."

The conditions Messiaen describes were not perhaps ideal
for composing. They may, however, have been ideal for
listening. That "diverse class of society," desperate for a
crumb of hope, hearts atremble, could have been the same
poor-in-spirit crowd Christ gazed upon as he delivered the
Sermon on the Mount.

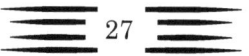

FRANCIS THOMPSON

Francis Thompson (1859-1907), English author, ascetic, and drug addict, wrote "The Hound of Heaven"—a poem about God's relentless pursuit of the human soul that is to this day known and recited world-wide.

Thompson was born into a middle-class Catholic family from Preston, Lancashire. His father was a provincial doctor; his mother died during Thompson's boyhood. Wishing to please his father, he entered Owens College (now the University of Manchester) to study medicine at the age of 18 but loathed the coursework and eventually quit.

While at Manchester, he suffered a nervous breakdown and began taking opium to calm himself. In London, where he moved at 26, he became addicted. For three years he was nearly destitute, wandering the streets doing odd jobs—selling matches, calling cabs, assisting bootmakers—to support his drug habit.

For a time he was homeless, sleeping on the streets of Charing Cross. He later credited a prostitute who befriended and sheltered him during this period as an angel who had saved his life.

Thompson had always been drawn to writing and, also during this time, managed to send some poems to the magazine *Merrie England*. Wilfrid and Alice Meynell, the magazine's editors, spotted his promise, hunted him down, and took him under their wing. They paid for two years of medical treatment at Our Lady of England Priory, Storrington. Thompson's addiction abated, though he never entirely recovered.

His first book, *Poems*, published in 1893, included the immortal "The Hound of Heaven."

The book was well-received. Other poetry collections followed. His selected prose includes *Health and Holiness* and *The Life of St. Ignatius*.

If not widely read during his lifetime, neither was Thompson altogether unnoticed as a writer. Wilfrid Meynell called him "a poet of high thinking, of 'celestial vision', and of imaginings that found literary images of answering splendor." The Catholic apologist G.K. Chesterton deemed him "a great poet."

The Victorian poet-critic Coventry Patmore, called "The Hound of Heaven" "one of the very few great odes of which the language can boast."

No matter how often heard, the poem's opening lines still raise a shiver:

"I fled Him, down the nights and down the days;
I fled Him, down the arches of the years;
I fled Him, down the labyrinthine ways
Of my own mind; and in the mist of tears
I hid from Him..."

As we converts especially know—good luck. God will not be mocked.

A lifetime of ill health took its toll. Near the end, Thompson was cared for by the Sisters of St. John and St. Elizabeth. He died at 47 of consumption and was buried at St. Mary's Catholic Cemetery in London's Kensal Green. His tombstone is inscribed with the last line of a poem he wrote for a godson: "Look for me in the nurseries of Heaven."

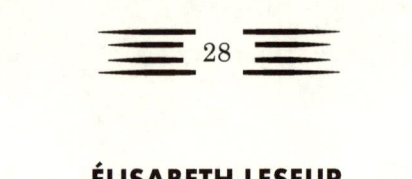

ÉLISABETH LESEUR

Élisabeth Leseur (1866-1914), married French laywoman, was a noted spiritual writer, consoler and friend.

Her husband, Félix, a doctor, lost his Catholic faith shortly before their 1889 wedding and became a publicly vocal atheist.

Ironically, the suffering she endured as a result invited her to a deeper exploration of her own, until then rather conventional, faith. Over time, she saw that enduring the anti-Catholic jibes of her husband, whom she loved deeply, could be a hidden form of mortification. "Silence is sometimes an act of energy," she observed, "and smiling, too."

But Leseur was no retiring faux-martyr. A lively hostess, she carried out her social duties as a member of Paris's wealthy bourgeois with grace and good humor. A loyal friend, she carried on a wide-ranging spiritual correspondence— mostly unbeknownst to her husband—for the duration of her marriage.

All the while, she continued to develop a rich and hidden interior life: her collected journals are now widely considered a spiritual classic.

Her entry for May 3, 1904, is typical: "Has my life known any unhappier time than this?...And yet through all these trials and in spite of the lack of interior joy, there is a deep place that all these waves of sorrow cannot touch."

In a world that so often despises Christ, his Church, and those of us who, however falteringly, try to follow him, Leseur is a powerful example. She wrote: "We must never reject anyone who seeks to approach us spiritually; perhaps that person, consciously or unconsciously, is in quest of the 'unknown God' (Acts 17: 23) and has sensed in us something that reveals his presence; perhaps he or she thirsts for truth and feels that we live by this truth."

"Look around oneself for proud sufferers in need, find them, and give them the alms of our heart, of our time, and of our tender respect."

"I know by experience that in hours of trial certain graces are obtained for others, which all our efforts had not hitherto obtained. I have thus come to the conclusion that suffering is a higher form of action, the highest expression of the wonderful Communion of Saints."

In frail health all her life, by July, 1913, Leseur was bedridden with the breast cancer to which she would succumb the following year. In the silence of her heart, she made the decision to offer up all her sufferings for the conversion of her husband's soul.

After she died, Félix found among her papers a letter she had written to him revealing her fervent prayers that he would turn to Christ and become a priest. Outraged, he set off for Lourdes in the hopes of debunking what he considered to be the crank miracles that occurred there. Instead, at the Lourdes grotto he had a conversion experience.

As the French say, "Woman's will, God's will." Félix was ordained a Dominican priest in 1923. He spent much of his last twenty-seven years promulgating the writings, and advancing the cause for beatification, of his treasured late wife.

29

BLESSED BENEDICT DASWA

Benedict Daswa (1946-1990), South African schoolteacher, principal, and martyr, fell victim to a murderous mob for refusing to fund their anti-Catholic witchcraft causes.

He was born Tshimangadzo Samuel Daswa in the village of Mbahe in Limpopo: the northernmost—and poorest—province in South Africa. His parents were of the Lemba tribe, sometimes referred to as "Black Jews" because of their adherence to Jewish laws and traditions. When his father unexpectedly died, it fell to him—the eldest of five children—to support and encourage the education of his younger siblings.

He worked for a time as a herd boy and developed a love of gardening. While visiting with an uncle in Johannesburg, he was introduced to Catholicism. He converted in 1963. Inspired by the Benedictine motto *ora et labora* (pray and work), he took the name Benedict upon his baptism and was confirmed three months later.

He attended a teaching college near his hometown and earned a teacher's certificate there.

In 1974, he married Shadi Eveline Monyai. The couple had eight children.

In his village of Mbahe, Daswa became a community leader, catechist, and mentor to many young students. He became principal of Nweli Primary School and helped build the first Catholic church in the area. He gave produce from his garden to the needy and allowed students who were unable to pay their fees to work in the garden in order to earn their tuition.

Highly respected for his integrity and wisdom, he was secretary of the Headman's council and a popular Master of Ceremonies at local functions.

In late 1989 and early 1990, a series of gale-force storms, accompanied by lightning, occurred in the village. The elders of the community decided that "magic" was at play and demanded a tax from each resident to ferret out and destroy the witch who had caused them. Believing the storms were a natural phenomenon, and unwilling to support anti-Catholic superstition, Benedict Daswa argued against their decision and refused to pay the tax. The elders perceived this as an insult to village tradition and customs.

On February 2, 1990, he drove a sister-in-law and her sick child to a doctor in a neighboring town. He was ambushed on his way home. The mob stoned, beat, stabbed, and clubbed him, then poured boiling water into his ears and nostrils. His last words were reportedly "God, into your hands receive my spirit."

35,000 people attended Daswa's funeral. His mother later converted and saved her pension earnings in order to buy a tombstone for her son.

His beatification Mass took place at Limpopo on September 13, 2015. Cardinal Angelo Amato presided on behalf of Pope Francis. Deputy President Cyril Ramaphosa observed, "He paid the ultimate price for his beliefs on the same day that the then President FW de Klerk announced the unbanning of our liberation movements and the release of our beloved Nelson Mandela."

Blessed Daswa is the first South African in the history of the Church to be recognized as a martyr of Christ.

30

MARSHALL McLUHAN

Herbert Marshall McLuhan (1911-1980), author of *Understanding Media: The Extensions of Man* (1964), coined the prescient phrase: "The Medium is the Message." Widely acknowledged as a seminal philosopher and writer about the cultural effect of media, McLuhan was a convert, an almost daily communicant, and an ardent Catholic.

Born in Canada to Protestant parents, he attended the University of Manitoba and did graduate work at Cambridge University.

He moved to the U.S., taught at the university level, and entered the Church in 1937 at the age of 26. "I came in on my knees," he later observed. "That is the only way in."

In 1939, he married Corinne Lewis. The couple raised six children. His son Eric McLuhan recalls, "We said the Rosary as a family before retiring to bed most nights."

The man who has been called variously the father of media

studies, a communications theorist, and a prophet of the information age did not publicly discuss his religion. "People who can see don't walk around saying, 'I'm seeing things' all day," he once noted. "They simply see the world."

Though charismatic and engaging, McLuhan had little use for academia, once telling an interlocuter: "I have no theories whatever about anything. I make observations by way of discovering contours, lines of force, and pressures."

His great area of exploration was the process by which human perception is trained. He defined medium broadly. A light bulb, for example, is a medium "that creates an environment by its mere presence." Media, he believed, act as "technological extensions of our body." "The medium is the message" refers to the fact that the medium by which a message is conveyed influences the way the message is perceived.

McLuhan predated the dawn of cyberspace. But his theory that media affect how we view and experience the world—and thus, eventually, interpersonal relationships and even religious experiences—could hardly be more relevant to contemporary times.

"The content of any medium is always another medium," he proposed. One content of today's social media, for example, is photos: of ourselves, our pets, our friends. But the message of that content is narcissism: we're a culture obsessed with watching others look at us as we look at ourselves in the mirror.

To the end, religion was the ground of McLuhan's life. His faith sustained him after a 1979 stroke. He died in his sleep on December 31, 1980.

McLuhan was no Luddite. But he did recognize that the real content of any given medium is the person who uses it. He observed:

> "There is a deep-seated repugnance in the human breast against understanding the processes in which we are involved. Such understanding involves far too much responsibility for our actions."

The world becomes ever more addicted to virtual reality, a pale and pathetic perversion of the Way, the Truth and the Life. There is one medium that contains no other medium, that is irreducible, that is the Alpha and Omega. That would be the Real Body and the Real Blood of Jesus Christ.

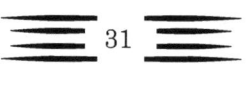

31

MARIA YUDINA

Maria Yudina (1899-1970), Russian pianist, was openly
Catholic under Communism, a "holy fool" who gave her
money to the poor and once responded to a middle-of-the-
night summons by Stalin to play Mozart's Concerto No. 23.

Born to a Jewish family in the town of Nevel, in the
western part of Russia, she converted to the Russian-
Orthodox church in 1919. She was dismissed from the
Petrograd Conservatory in 1930 for replying "Yes" when
asked whether she believed in God. She wore a large cross
while performing in public, a demonstration of faith that,
in Communist Russia, could easily have earned her a death
sentence.

She was notorious for going without food, pampering her
cats, and practicing the piano in a frigid apartment. When
friends once pitched in to help her fix a broken window, she
immediately gave the money away.

Testimony: The Memoirs of Dmitri Shostakovich is a rich source of Yudina anecdotes. The composer, a contemporary and colleague, seemed simultaneously exasperated, bewildered, and in awe of this "marvelous musician."

"Yudina was a strange person, and very much a loner," he wrote. "Strange things kept happening to her." "Yudina saw music in a mystical light. For instance, she saw Bach's Goldberg Variations "as a series of illustrations to the Holy Bible," he observed. "She always played as though she were giving a sermon."

"I had the impression that Yudina wore the same black dress during her entire long life, it was so worn and soiled."

Shostakovich describes the famous Mozart Concert incident like this:

> "In his final years, Stalin seemed more and more like a madman, and I think his superstition grew. The "Leader and Teacher" sat locked up in one of his many dachas, amusing himself in bizarre ways...[He] didn't let anyone in to see him for days at a time. He listened to the radio a lot. Once Stalin called the Radio Committee, where the administration was, and asked if they had a record of Mozart's Piano Concerto no. 23, which had been heard on the radio the day before. 'Played by Yudina,' he added. They told Stalin that of course they had it. Actually, there was

*no record, the concert had been live. But they were afraid
to say no to Stalin, no one ever knew what the consequences
might be. A human life meant nothing to him.*

*Stalin demanded that they send the record with Yudina's
performance of the Mozart to his dacha. The committee
panicked, but they had to do something. They called in
Yudina and an orchestra and recorded that night. Everyone
was shaking with fright, except for Yudina, naturally. But
she was a special case, that one, the ocean was only knee-
deep for her."*

Soon after, Yudina received an envelope with twenty
thousand rubles. She was told it came on the express orders
of Stalin. In reply she wrote him a letter that, according to
Shostakovich, went something like this:

*"I thank you, Joseph Vissarionovich, for your aid. I will
pray for you day and night and ask the Lord to forgive your
great sins before the people and the country. The Lord is
merciful and He'll forgive you.* I gave the money to
the church that I attend."

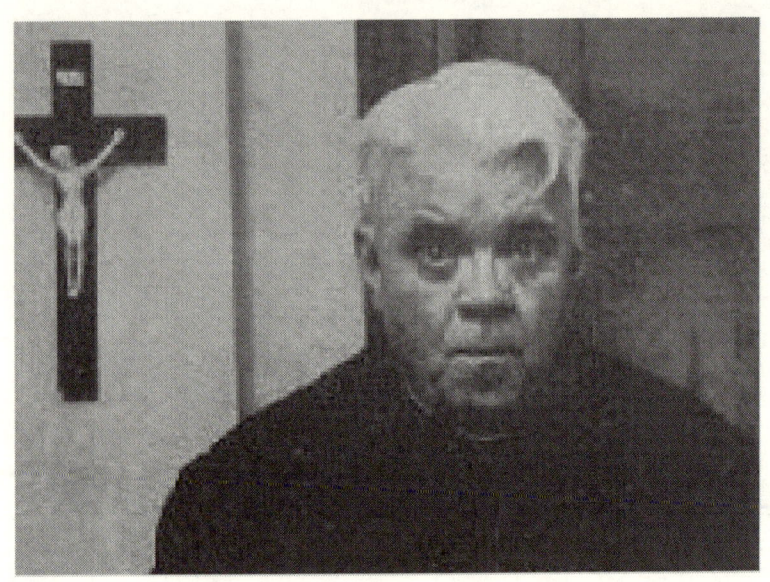

 32

FATHER ED DOWLING

Fr. Edward Dowling, sj (1898-1960), the oldest of five children born to a devout Irish Catholic family from St. Louis, became a beloved Jesuit priest. Though not himself an alcoholic, he was a close friend and spiritual advisor to Bill Wilson, co-founder of Alcoholics Anonymous.

An avid baseball player and newspaper reporter, Fr. Dowling entered the Jesuit seminary at Florissant, Missouri, in 1919. While there, he was diagnosed with the arthritis from which he would suffer crippling pain for the remainder of his life.

Starting in 1929, he studied theology at St. Mary's College in Kansas. Upon being ordained in 1931, he became associate editor at *The Queen's Work*, the magazine of the Jesuit-sponsored Sodalities of Our Lady in St. Louis—a post he held until his death.

Fr. Dowling's religious leanings can be discerned from a widely-circulated quote from a piece in the *Chicago Daily News* dated July 28, 1941: "The two greatest obstacles to democracy in the United States are, first, the widespread delusion among the poor that we have a democracy, and second, the chronic terror among the rich, lest we get it."

He embraced the cross of daily life with good cheer, a kind
word, a sense of humor. When his desk buzzer once broke, he
took to using a cap gun to summon his secretary. In his work
to honor the black community, he used his genealogical skills
to locate the previously unmarked grave of Dred Scott. He
had a deep feel for all of humanity.

When a drinking friend from Chicago lost his wife, Fr.
Dowling took him to a meeting of Alcoholics Anonymous, in
those days a fledgling organization. Noting the similarity
of AA principles—surrender to a Higher Power, rigorous
honesty, a daily examination of conscience—to Ignatian
spirituality, he applied those same principles to the
sacrament of marriage and founded what would come to be
known as Cana Conferences. His tone was matter-of-fact and
friendly. He helped found Recovery Inc. for neurotics. He
applied the AA principles to his own compulsive tendencies
to overeat and smoke.

He traveled exhaustively. In 1940, he arrived unannounced
at Bill Wilson's walk-up flat in New York. The maintenance
man who let Fr. Ed in took him for a bum. He climbed the
stairs to the second floor in spite of the chronic pain in his
leg, rather than make Wilson come down to him.

The two became devoted, life-long friends, with Fr. Dowling
in the role of spiritual advisor. "Father Ed, an early and
wonderful friend of AA, died as this last message went to

press," Wilson wrote in the spring of 1960. "He was the greatest and most gentle soul to walk this planet. I was closer to him than to any other human being on earth."

He was an old-school priest, made of the kind of fine cloth that prefers to disguise itself as sacking. His funeral Mass was thronged. From society matrons in mink coats to Skid Row drunks, people came from around the country to pay homage.

"I really haven't done anything," Fr. Dowling once said. "It's really simple. I just happened to be around."

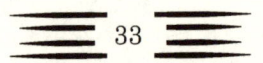

BLESSED
CHARLES DE FOUCAULD

Fr. Charles de Foucauld (1858–1916) lived among, and died at the hands of, the Tuareg in the Algerian Sahara.

Born into French nobility, as a young man Foucauld was a playboy. While serving in the French army, he kept a mistress named Mimi.

He left the military in 1882, underwent a conversion in 1886, and joined the Cistercian Trappists, first in France, then in Akbès, Syria. He learned the Arab language and was ordained a priest at the age of 43 in 1901. He built a hermitage in the Tamanrasset region of Southern Algeria, desiring to serve the poorest and most abandoned.

In May, 1904, he wrote "I offer my life for the conversion of the Tuareg, the Moroccans, all the people of the Sahara, all the infidels."

His asceticism was so extreme, however, that virtually no-one was able to follow him. He lived almost exclusively on couscous and dates, wore a torn, stained tunic, and cut his own hair and beard without the aid of a mirror. He rose fifteen minutes before everyone else to say Mass in the frigid desert mornings, worked inhuman hours, barely slept, and suffered variously from scurvy, fever, neuralgia, and emaciation.

Yet "Each Mass is like Christmas, and charity is more important than poverty," he realized.

The little man with a sharp graying beard and a blood-red cross sewn to the front of his dingy tunic was a compelling, if paradoxical, figure.

He was a contemplative with a militaristic, even fanatical streak; a humble, self-effacing monk who lived entirely for God and who was also a fervent French nationalist.

He could write, "[Our mission is] to regard every human being as a beloved brother…Jesus has taught us to go like lambs amongst wolves, not to take up arms." In the next breath, he could say, of a Senoussi warrior who had killed several French soldiers: "I would catch the villain, stand him up immediately against a wall—and plug twelve bullets into his skin."

He could be impatient and jealous. Even his admirers admitted he was a romantic who loved mankind but found individual human relationships difficult.

As he aged, he suffered from loneliness. He felt his strength ebbing. In all his years in the desert, he had made not a single convert.

He was shot in the head by a 15-year-old Tuareg boy during a bungled robbery. His rosary, hand-drawn stations of the cross, and tabernacle containing the Host were found in the sand near his fort.

But after his death, stray followers began to appear. Today, the Association of the Brothers and Sisters of the Sacred Heart of Jesus, the Little Brothers of Jesus and several other religious congregations claim Foucauld as their founder.

He was beatified by Benedict XVI in November, 2005. In *The Sword and the Cross*, author Fergus Fleming notes: "[Many] testified to the strange powers of [Foucauld's] presence; describing it as something he did not exert but which simply emanated from his very being. Today, cynics might call it the power of fanaticism. In medieval times it would have been called a halo."

34

SOFIA CAVALLETTI

Sofia Cavalletti (1917-2011), co-foundress of the
Cathechesis of the Good Shepherd, developed a three-level,
nine-year method of religious education for children based on
Montessori principles.

A native of Rome and a Hebrew scholar, Cavalletti had
no background in, and no real contact with children's
education, until she was in her 30s.

But her own love of learning developed early. Taught at
home to read, she later wrote: "This still makes me so happy
and grateful to [my mother] for having put in my hands such
a precious tool. I remember that, when for the first time I
could read a little story by myself, I was so happy that I gave
to Mommy all my money—that is to say, three coins that did
not reach the value of one lire."

Under the tutelage of Dr. Eugenio Zolli, the former chief
rabbi of Rome and a Catholic convert, Cavalletti learned that

she had an affinity for languages. For the next fifty years, she went to the library every day to study. She also read Hebrew—in which she eventually earned a doctorate—daily.

Asked by a colleague in 1954 to teach a religion class to young people, Cavalletti encountered a child who would change her life: seven-year-old Paolo. Initially lukewarm about the prospect of studying Scripture, upon hearing Cavalletti's reading of Genesis, Paolo cried.

Those tears of joy amazed her. She intuitively understood that every child has a deep capacity for and wonder about God, attributes that she came to believe should be watered and fed like tender plants.

Through a teacher named Gianna Gobbi, Cavalletti learned Montessori principles: the child's natural capacity for reflection, love of order and silence, and delight in work. The children could learn from her, Cavalletti discovered, and— equally important—she could learn from them.

Together, Cavalletti and Gobbi observed the ways of teaching that generated the most interest and joy in the children. After years of trial and error, together they established what is now known as the Catechesis of the Good Shepherd, a method that has changed very little to this day.

Their goal was "To involve adults and children in a religious experience in which the religious values of the child are predominant, keeping in mind that the contemplative nature of the child indicates to the adult a certain way of drawing near to God."

Cavalletti preserved the biblical content of her teaching by focusing heavily on parables, which she understood connect the reality of our daily lives to the supernatural and the eternal in a way that platitudes, rules and formulae never can.

In lieu of a classroom, she and Gobbi developed a space they called an atrium, a space for combined learning and worship.

At 89, Cavalletti was still teaching children every Monday in one of the three atria she had established in her own home.

She died at 94. The Catechesis of the Good Shepherd has spread to at least 37 countries around the world.

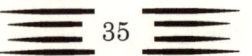

SERVANT OF GOD
CARDINAL FRANÇOIS-XAVIER
NGUYỄN VĂN THUẬN

Cardinal François-Xavier Nguyễn Văn Thuận (1928-2002) spent twelve years in prison under the Communists, nine of those in solitary confinement, praying for his tormentors.

A nephew of South Vietnam's first president, Ngô Đình Diệm, Cardinal Văn Thuận was born in Hue, entered the seminary in 1941 as an adolescent, and was ordained a priest in 1953.

He was appointed coadjutor archbishop of Saigon on April 24, 1975. Six days later, the city fell to the Communists. Because of his ties to the government, and his Catholicism, he was arrested and sent to a "re-education camp."

In his prison cell, he made a tiny Bible out of paper scraps, fashioned a crucifix from bits of wood and wire smuggled in by sympathetic guards, and on the backs of old calendars, wrote messages of hope and strength that a young boy whose help he had solicited copied out and distributed to members of the faithful outside the prison.

He took a personal, loving interest in the prison guards, considering them part of his extended family. He taught them English, Latin, French, and catechetics.

The "10 Rules of Life" he devised include "I will have only one wisdom: the science of the cross," "I will speak one language and wear one uniform: charity," and "I will have one very special love: the Blessed Virgin Mary."

Other of his written works include *The Road of Hope* and *Prayers of Hope*.

Sr. Maria Thuận Nguyen of the Dominican Sisters of St. Cecilia, writes of Cardinal Văn Thuận's time in prison: "He turned the concentration camp into a cathedral and the palm of his hand into an altar. He turned his shirt pocket into a tabernacle and turned the darkness of the sleeping quarters into a dwelling place for Light Himself."

Cardinal Văn Thuận himself said of his years in prison that it was God's turn to speak and for him to listen, and that he was happy there.

He was released on the Feast of the Presentation of Our

Lady in 1988, exiled until 1991, and made an official of the
Roma Curia soon after by Pope John Paul II. He held the
post of president of the Pontifical Council for Justice and
Peace from 1998 to 2002, and was appointed to the College of
Cardinals in 2001.

His simplicity and humility were legendary. Kishore
Jayabalan, an official at the Pontifical Council for Justice
and Peace at the time, recalled their first meeting: "[Cardinal
Thuận] came in to see me unannounced and without any
fanfare; I didn't even recognize him and thought it was some
old priest who happened to work there coming to say hello. It
was only when I saw his pectoral cross that I realized who
he was."

At the completion of the diocesan phase of Cardinal Thuận's
cause for beatification, held in July, 2013, Pope Francis told
the Vietnamese delegation, "So many people have written
to tell of graces [received] and signs attributed to the
intercession of the Servant of God Cardinal Văn Thuận. We
thank the Lord for this venerable brother, son of the East,
who ended his earthly journey in the service of the Successor
of St. Peter."

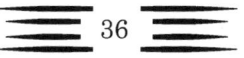

36

VENERABLE LUIGI ROCCHI

Luigi Rocchi (1932-1979) suffered from muscular
dystrophy and in spite of his complete physical debilitation,
became a widely-known consoler, spiritual advisor,
and friend.

Born in Rome, Rocchi moved north two years later
with his family to Tolentino, an industrial town in
the province of Macerata. He would live with his father, a
mechanic, and his mother, a homemaker, all his life.

Accounts vary as to when the first signs of his illness
appeared. What is known is that decreasing mobility
and a series of falls would lead him to leave high school.
Confined to a wheelchair by the age of 20, his dreams of
marriage and family crushed, he entered into a long period of
spiritual crisis. By 28, his hands and feet paralyzed, he was
completely immobile.

Later, he would write of that time:

> *"About eight years ago I found an old crucifix, broken and dirty. I had it repaired and cleaned up, the wood refreshed with oil. I hung it in my bedroom. One night, tormented by grief and the restraints of my illness, I spoke with him. I talked to him, he talked to me ....Suddenly the crucifix set off an intense light that filled the room and penetrated my heart, giving me a deep peace and an unmatched serenity. From that day I seem to have been released from a dark forest. I always felt a great inner joy and the desire to pass on to others the knowledge of God and his message of love."*

Confined to his bed, he received an endless stream of visitors seeking direction and consolation. With the aid of a stick attached to his forehead, he pecked out over 1700 letters of spiritual guidance on his trusty typewriter.

Accompanied by his mother, who served as nurse and attendant, he was able to make two pilgrimages: one to Lourdes, to pray for his suffering friends around the world, and one to Loreto, to visit the home of the Blessed Mother.

Every night his mother told him, "Luigino, Jesus loves you."

He referred to the poor and oppressed of the Third World as "living crucifixes," and joined his suffering to theirs. All who knew him were struck by his good cheer, even gaiety.

Monsignor Capovilla, secretary to Pope John XXIII, observed, "He has been appreciated and his house has become one great house of spirituality."

Monsignor Ersilio Tonino, archbishop of Macerata and Ravenna, wrote of him:

"I have known him very well and I have been immediately spellbound by him. Two aspects particularly struck me, Luigi's serenity and his desire not to be pitied. Luigi had a great gift, a liberty of spirit—a liberty of the mind. I have never seen anyone as happy as he. But there is another characteristic, the need to share his happiness, to encourage others in a deep relationship with God, for them to find happiness in pain...I can say that Luigi was one of the most beautiful souls I have ever met in my life."

"What is the secret of my joy?" Rocchi once remarked. "I am thirsty for God. So much thirst for God."

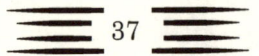

MOTHER ANTONIA BRENNER

Antonia Brenner (1926-2013), former Beverly Hills socialite and foundress of the Eudist Servants of the Eleventh Hour, ministered to and lived with the inmates at La Mesa, a notorious maximum-security prison in Tijuana, Mexico.

Born Mary Clark in Los Angeles, Brenner was the middle of three children. Her mother died giving birth to the fourth child. Her father ran a successful office supply business.

A marriage at 19 ended quickly in divorce. Her second marriage, to Carl Brenner, lasted 25 years and yielded seven children.

While married and living in Beverly Hills, California, Brenner was active in charity work. In the 1960s, a priest invited her to visit La Mesa. She began distributing aspirin, toilet paper, and prescription eyeglasses to thieves, rapists and murderers.

After her second divorce she moved to San Diego, which made visiting the prison easier. When her youngest child, Antony, reached adolescence, she made the wrenching decision to cede custody to Brenner, gave away her belongings, and in 1977 moved to Tijuana in order to be near the inmates.

In her early years of volunteering at La Mesa, Brenner took informal vows and sewed her own habit. According to the website of the Eudist Servants of the Eleventh Hour, "After a year, her service to prisoners came to the attention of Bishop Juan Jesus Posadas of Tijuana and Bishop Leo Maher of neighboring San Diego. She was officially welcomed and blessed by both Bishops: Bishop Maher made her an auxiliary to him while Bishop Posadas made her an auxiliary Mercedarian, an order which has a special devotion to prisoners. At age fifty, she had become a sister."

Around the same time, she moved into the prison, taking a cell in the women's section.

In a 1982 interview with the *Los Angeles Times*, Brenner said, "Something happened to me when I saw men behind bars. ... When I left, I thought a lot about the men. When it was cold, I wondered if the men were warm; when it was raining, if they had shelter. I wondered if they had medicine and how their families were doing... You know, when I returned to the prison to live, I felt as if I'd come home."

Petite, indefatigable in her black and white habit, she lived in a 10 by 10 cell as one of the inmates. She ate the same prison fare and with the members of her flock, lined up for morning roll call.

Around 1997, she founded the Eudist Servants of the Eleventh Hour for older women with a desire to serve the poor. In 2003 the Bishop of Tijuana formally approved the community.

"Pleasure depends on where you are, who you are with, what you are eating," she once observed. "Happiness is different. Happiness does not depend on where you are. I live in prison. And I have not had a day of depression in 25 years. I have been upset, angry. I have been sad. But never depressed. I have a reason for my being."

She was known to the prison inmates as "La Mama." A 2005 biography by Mary Jordan and Kevin Sullivan is called *Prison Angel*.

Mother Antonia died of natural causes at 86 in her Tijuana home.

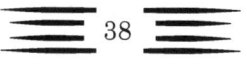 38

FRANZ WRIGHT

Franz Wright (1953-2015), Pulitzer Prize-winning
poet and Catholic convert, struggled with addiction and
depression and wrote movingly of isolation, illness, and
religious transcendence.

His work includes the poetry collections *God's Silence*
(2006); *Wheeling Motel* (2009); *Kindertotenwald* (2011);
and *F* (2013). He won the Pulitzer in 2004 for *Walking to
Martha's Vineyard* (2001).

Wright was born in Vienna, Austria, to the poet James
Wright and his wife Liberty (now Kovacs), an American-born
daughter of Greek immigrants who later became a nurse.

The elder Wright suffered from alcoholism and manic-
depression, and the marriage was tempestuous. As a child
Wright was exposed through his father to such literary
luminaries as Theodore Roethke, Saul Bellow and Robert
Bly. His parents divorced when he was 8. His mother

remarried a man who was physically abusive.

As a poet, Wright taught at various universities, held down jobs in mental health clinics, and worked as a volunteer to grieving children. He was also hospitalized himself on several occasions for depression and alcoholism.

In 1999, he married the American translator Elizabeth Oehlkers Wright. He also attained sobriety that year and converted to Roman Catholicism.

In an interview with American poet and critic Ernest Hilbert entitled "The Secret Glory" and published in 2006, Wright was asked, "Must one feel extremes of pain or love to create authentic poetry, or is stylistic capacity enough?"

He replied, "You must have both, clearly. And have them to a terrible, excruciating and obsessive degree." "Religion seems to be central to your writing," Hilbert continued. "Can you say a few words about how religion has affected your life and your view of the world?"

"My religious faith is very real and literal, almost to a childlike degree—though with my ancient skepticism and dread of abandonment thrown in—and I can only say it has made it possible for me to go on living. I would not have been able to go on living otherwise."

Critic Helen Vender observed in the *New York Review of Books*, "Wright's scale of experience...runs from the homicidal to the ecstatic."

Chicago Tribune cultural critic Julia Keller wrote that *Kindertotenwald* [loosely translated as "forest of dead children"] is "ultimately about joy and grace and the possibility of redemption, about coming out whole on the other side of emotional catastrophe."

Novelist Denis Johnson said of Wright's book *Entry in an Unknown Hand*: "These poems break me, they're like tiny jewels shaped by blunt, ruined fingers—miraculous gifts."

Of winning the Pulitzer, Wright said, "I consider it a great honor, and it still amazes me, and I think it will always amaze me." His father also won the Pulitzer for poetry.

Wright died of cancer at his home in Waltham Massachusetts in May, 2015. He was 62. "Soon, soon," he wrote in "Nude With Handgun and Rosary," "between one instant and the next, you will be well."

SERVANT OF GOD
DOROTHY DAY

Dorothy Day (1897-1980), widely hailed as the most influential Catholic laywoman of the 20th century, co-founded the lay Catholic Worker movement.

By 1932, Dorothy's checkered past—the Bohemian nightlife, the flirtation with Communism, the abortion, the common-law marriage—was behind her. After converting to Catholicism in 1927, she'd left Forster Batterham, the love of her life, because of his refusal to sanction the baptism of the daughter they'd conceived together. The separation was wrenching, the hardest thing, she later said, that she would ever do.

On the feast of the Immaculate Conception of that year, she visited the National Shrine in Washington, DC, and prayed that "some way would be opened for me to work for the poor and the oppressed."

When she returned to New York City, the French peasant-intellectual Peter Maurin was waiting on her doorstep.

On May 1, 1933, the Catholic Worker was born: first a newspaper, then a Bowery soup kitchen, then the first "house of hospitality" from which a worldwide lay movement would eventually blossom.

Peter Maurin's role was to "enunciate principles"; Dorothy's was to implement them. She railed against our "dirty rotten system": an economy based on war, the rich who fed off the poor. Her vision of a new system was based on sacrifice, penance, prayer, personalism, and pacifism.

During the Second Vatican Council she took a steamer to Rome and fasted for peace. She suffered many stints of civil-disobedience jail time with no complaint and none of the self-promoting breast-beating that takes place on today's social media. She sheltered, fed, and lived with the marginalized and the crazy. Her compassion was for others, not herself; for those who are poor not voluntarily but involuntarily: poor in spirit, poor in choices, poor in inner resources.

She built her life on a bedrock of daily devotions: the Divine Office, rosaries, vigils, prayer, fasts, and always, the Mass. For all her radicalism, she was as observant as any medieval nun. For all her social activism, she was at heart a mystic.

"Physical and spiritual senses need to be 'mortified,' subdued, disciplined," she observed. That was at the age of 78.

In between, she wrote: essays, editorials, letters, her autobiography, *The Long Loneliness*. She was offered (and turned down) 12 honorary doctorates. The cause for her canonization is underway.

But perhaps the highest accolade was conferred by Mr. Breen, a cantankerous "guest," given to hurling racial epithets, who arrived at the NY House of Hospitality in his seventies. "I am at my wits end," wrote Dorothy to a friend in July, 1935. "He sits at the lower window like a Cerberus and growls and curses at everyone who comes in for a bite of food or for some clothing...And he, after all, is Christ."

Mr. Breen stayed until his death, in 1939.

"As long as I live," he once wrote her, "I shall always be proud of having had you as my boss and my friend. Your little glimpses into my mind on personal responsibility a few days ago remade me and I have, thank you, ceased to hate people as I was wont to."

 40

JEAN-HENRI FABRÉ

Jean-Henri Fabré (1823-1915), a French scientist known for his study of and love for insects, wrote several books. Among them is the 1921 classic, *Fabré's Book of Insects*, with color plates by E.J. Detmold.

The glow-worm, the locust, the mason-wasp: all our favorite insect friends are here.

An ardent Catholic with a deep sense of God's design, Fabré wrote with the conviction of the self-taught and a sly sense of humor. "Others again have reproached me with my style, which has not the solemnity, nay, better, the dryness of the schools," he observed. "They fear lest a page that is read without fatigue should not always be the expression of the truth."

In the introduction to his *Book of Insects*, he told as a boy of coming upon the nest of a "lovely bird" that held six eggs of a "magnificent azure blue, very bright." He took one and, walking carefully home, met a priest who identified the egg as belonging to a Saxicola, then gently chided the young Fabré for his cruelty.

Fabré continued: "From the conversation I learnt two things: first, that robbing birds' nests is cruel, and secondly, that birds and beasts have names just like ourselves."

As an adult, Fabré and his own young son would steal out in the dead of night with cardboard boxes, torches, nets, magnifying glasses, spades, and rulers. They gathered eggs, nests, and larvae to bring home, experiment with, and study.

Darwin called Fabré, who made his living by teaching geometry and chemistry, "the incomparable observer." Though Fabré greatly admired Darwin, he did not subscribe to his theories, preferring instead to bow to mystery. Using his own sui generis love for studying insects as an example, he wrote:

"Of scientific education...I have none whatsoever. I never set foot in a lecture hall except to endure the ordeal of examinations. Without masters, without guides, often without books, in spite of poverty, that terrible extinguisher, I went ahead, persisted, facing my difficulties, until the indomitable bump ended by shedding its scanty contents. I was a born animalist. Why and how? No reply."

He learned that the insect world is full of skilled surgeons, expert anesthesiologists, master mathematicians, martyrs, Christ-figures, and criminals.

"For all her sanctimonious airs, the [praying mantis] is a cannibal. She will eat her sister...Indeed, she even makes a habit of devouring her mate, whom she seizes by the neck and then swallows by little mouthfuls."

The Spanish Copris, a beetle, by contrast, "slips in and out of the narrow spaces between the cradles [of her grubs], inspecting them with the utmost care. If I disturb her she sometimes rubs the tip of her body against the edge of the wing-cases, making a soft rustling sound, like a murmur of complaint. In this way, caring industriously for her cradles, and sometimes snatching a brief sleep beside them, the mother waits."

The "Homer of the Insect World" lived out his days in a small house in Provence

"After eighty-seven years of thought and observation," he wrote near the end, "I say not merely that I believe in God—I can even say that I see him."

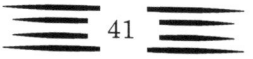

SISTER LEONELLA SGORBATI

Leonella Sgorbati (1940–2006), an Italian Roman Catholic nun, became a martyr in Mogadishu, Somalia, shortly after comments made by Pope Benedict XVI concerning Islam.

Born near Piacenza, Leonella heard the missionary call during adolescence. At the request of her mother, she waited until she was 20, then joined the Consolata Missionary Sisters.

She attended nursing school in England from 1966 to 1968. Appointed to Kenya, she arrive in 1970, took her perpetual vows in November, 1972, and from 1993 to 1999, served there as the Consolata Missionary Sisters' regional superior.

After three decades in Kenya, Sr. Leonalla took a sabbatical year during which she investigated the possibility of opening a nursing school in the SOS Children's Village Hospital in Mogadishu, the capital of Somalia.

The military-run government of Somalia had effectively collapsed in 1991. The political situation there was dangerous and unstable. Sister Leonella forged on.

In 2002, her dream was realized. The nursing school opened in Mogadishu with Sr. Leonella at the helm. Her first students graduated in 2006. After much bureaucratic red tape she managed to travel with three of them to Kenya where, hoping to prepare them to serve as future tutors, she enrolled them at the Medical Training School.

She went on to Uganda, scouting for prospective nursing students there as well. She had great difficulty returning to Mogadishu. Islamic courts now had control of the Somalian government and had enacted strict rules governing foreign travelers. Moreover, remarks about Islam recently made by then Pope Benedict XVI had infuriated certain radical Somali clerics. Nonetheless, Sr. Leonella managed to return on September 13, 2006.

On September 17, as Sr. Leonella walked across the street from the hospital to the convent for lunch, two gunmen emerged from behind taxis and kiosks and opened fire. Her Somalian bodyguard, Mohamed Osman Mahamud, shot back. The gunmen killed him and shot Sr. Leonella twice, once in the thigh, once in the back, severing a major artery.

She was rushed to the hospital and, as she lay dying, is reported to have said, "Perdono; perdono." ("I forgive; I forgive."). She was 70.

Shortly afterward, the then Holy Father, Pope Emeritus Benedict XVI, gave a public address in which he said:

"This sister, who for many years served the poor and the children in Somalia, died pronouncing the word 'forgive'... This is the most authentic Christian testimony, a peaceful sign of contradiction which shows the victory of love over hatred and evil."

The Consolata Missionary Sisters' website observes: "Sister Leonella was well aware of the danger surrounding her. As she used to say, she knew that there was a bullet with her name engraved on it just waiting for her in Mogadishu."

In October, 2008, the cross Sr. Leonella wore was transferred to the Basilica di San Bartolomeo all'Isola in Rome, the Memorial of the New Martyrs. It resides there, beside the relics of other Christian martyrs killed during the last century.

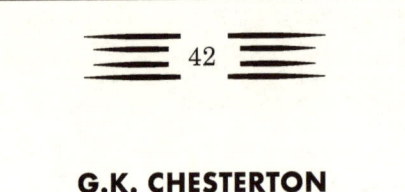

G.K. CHESTERTON

G. K. Chesterton (1874-1936), English writer, lay theologian, poet, and philosopher, converted to Catholicism in 1922 and became one of its greatest contemporary apologists.

His output was prodigious. He wrote over a hundred books—among them *Orthodoxy* and *The Everlasting Man*—as well as plays short stories, novels, poems, and over 4000 newspaper essays.

Corpulent, a lover of fine cigars, and notoriously absent-minded, Chesterton was said frequently to have called his wife Frances from a train station to ask where he was going.

He was also loyal, compassionate and kind. During a time when Frances was suffering from depression, he wrote to a friend to cancel a planned visit in favor of sitting by her side for a few nights. "One of the mysteries of marriage (which must be a Sacrament and an extraordinary one, too) is that a man evidently useless like me can yet become at certain instants indispensable," he wrote. "And the further oddity (which I invite you to explain on mystical grounds) is that he never feels so small as when he knows he is necessary."

Married 35 years, the couple remained childless.

Almost everything he wrote is quotable. All Chesterton fans have their favorites. "The Christian ideal has not been tried and found wanting. It has been found difficult; and left untried."

Courage means "a strong desire to live taking the form of a readiness to die."

"One can hardly think too little of one's self. One can hardly think too much of one's soul."

Chesterton gave us Christ as poet, a troubadour with a dashing spirit of adventure, the Man of Sorrows characterized by knightly courtesy and sublime class.

"The prince of paradox," as Chesterton was sometimes called, reminds us that there is not a scintilla of haughtiness, stodginess, or falsity in our Savior: "For some extraordinary reason, there is a fixed notion that it is more liberal to disbelieve in miracles than to believe in them. Why, I cannot imagine, nor can anybody tell me."

He posits that the *je ne sais quoi* element of Christ, that elusive characteristic upon which we can't quite put our finger, is mirth. Chesterton's extraordinary ability to convey the strangeness of Catholicism allows us to say, "Yes, that's just it!" He invites us to a great romance in which the stakes are life and death.

In fact, a single passage from his *St. Francis of Assisi* may well have been responsible for my own conversion. Rationalists, he noted, will find things like "the Stigmata a stumbling-block because to them religion was a philosophy."

But *"[A] man will not roll in the snow for a stream of tendency by which all things fulfil the law of their being. He will not go without food in the name of something, not ourselves, that makes for righteousness. He will do things like this, or pretty nearly like this, under quite a different impulse. He will do these things when he is in love...Tell it as the tale of one of the Troubadours, and the wild things he would do for his lady, and the whole of the modern puzzle disappears."*

FATHER SEBASTIAN KNEIPP

Fr. Sebastian Kneipp (1821-1897), Bavarian priest and a forefather of the naturopathic medicine movement, developed the "Kneipp Cure" form of hydrologoy. The basis of his thought was that the application of water through various methods, temperatures and pressures has therapeutic or healing effects.

Born to a family of weavers, at 21 Sebastian was poised to start his apprenticeship. "But since my childhood, something very different had been inscribed on the leaves of my heart," he later wrote. "With unspeakable pain and longing for the realization of my ideal, I had waited long, long years for this discharge: I wished to become a priest."

He began studying for the priesthood at the age of 23, and was ordained in 1852.

But in the early years of his studies, he suffered morally and physically, apparently from tuberculosis. He became a near invalid. Then he chanced upon "an insignificant little volume": a treatise on cold-water cure.

That little volume would both restore him to health and determine the course of his life.

Nestled in the Bavarian Alps, Fr. Kneipp undertook a regimen that included hot and cold water treatments, local plants and herbs, and plunging into the frigid waters of the Danube several times a week.

He was cured.

"Nature has provided us generously with everything we need to remain in good health," he maintained.

Fr. Kneipp considered the five elements of water, plants, exercise, nutrition, and balance—he called them "The Five Pillars"—to be closely interconnected and drew them together in a holistic life philosophy.

For a time, he recommended ice cold baths and walking barefoot in the snow. Eventually, he decided those treatments were too severe.

"Not until I incorporated the soul did I find success," Fr. Kneipp noted.

In 1886, he published a book called *My Water Cure*. His "Water Applications" included Affusions, Lavations, and Swathings. A treatment called "The Wet Shirt" acted as "a very mild form of blister."

In promoting the Hay-flower, Oat-straw, and Pine-tree baths, Fr. Kneipp noted: "How good God is towards us!... His paternal love makes countless little herbs spring up from the earth in order to bring solace and consolation to suffering mankind."

For sixteen years as parish priest, he practiced his healing arts from a town called Bad [Spa] Wörishofen. Whether the problem was infertility, bed-wetting, or cancer, the water cure, he maintained, could help. Thousands flocked, from Europe and beyond. Today the town is still dedicated to the Kneipp-Kur [Cure].

But Fr. Kneipp's goal was never to develop high-end spas for the rich. As the translator of *My Water Cure*, identified only as "A. de F," observed in 1891, "He specially prides himself on the simplicity of his cure, which renders it accessible to the poorest—and here lies his true vocation, helping the poor. While he is kind to every one, it is easy to see that his whole heart goes out to meet those who are in want."

DANTE ALIGHIERI

Dante Alighieri (1265-1321), Italian poet and moral philosopher, authored *The Divine Comedy*. His three-part journey through Hell, Purgatory, and Paradise, with the Latin poet Virgil as his guide and the ethereal figure of Beatrice as his muse, is perhaps the greatest work ever written on romantic love.

Dante started "The Inferno," his description through the nine circles of Hell, in 1307, five years after he was exiled from Florence on politically-motivated corruption charges. Apparently, he spent much of his life wandering between Bologna, Padua and possibly Paris.

Reams have been written about this iconic poem: Dante's innovative jettisoning of Latin in favor of the Italian vernacular, the *terza rima* that makes translating so fiendishly difficult, the debates over who has remained most faithful to the text: Ciardi? Sayers? Sinclair?

What we do know is that the poem was inspired when Dante met his real-life Beatrice on the streets of his native Florence.

In Religion and Love in Dante: The Theology of Romantic Love, Charles Williams describes her effect on him like this:

> *"The heart, where (to him) 'the spirit of life' dwelled, exclaimed to him, at that first meeting: 'Behold, a god stronger than I, who is to come and rule over me.' The brain declared: 'Now your beatitude has appeared to you.' And the liver (where natural emotions, such as sex, inhabited) said: 'O misery! How I shall be disturbed henceforward.'"*

If you've ever been in thrall to such a catastrophic attachment, you know you wouldn't wish it on your worst enemy. Part of the beauty of *The Divine Comedy* is that Dante assures us the experience is essentially religious: part passion, part pathology; half holy fire, half fires of hell.

The Divine Comedy is often described as a journey from sin to redemption. But in *Dark Wood to White Rose*, Dante scholar Helen M. Luke more rightly casts the journey described in the poem as a pilgrimage to transformed consciousness that at last allows us to know the "love which moves the sun and the other stars":

"The man who wrote the last canto of the *Paradiso* knew that we can never come to this vision by any shortcut. We cannot bypass the experience of Hell; and still less can we evade the long struggle of Purgatory, through which we come to maturity in love."

To meet the person who makes us feel as if we were simultaneously being brought electrically alive and killed—and to stay the course through the ensuing pilgrimage—is to embark on perhaps the most heroic and most perilous adventure of which a human being is capable.

That is the journey for which we were born, and for which there is no earthly guide, no familiar landmarks.

That is the adventure charted in Dante's masterwork.

Ecce homo—behold the man—said Pilate as he presented a bound and bloodied Christ. We, too, are called to die for love, standing silently on the pinnacle where suffering and joy meet: consenting to be crucified, holding fast to the Resurrection.

 45

SISTER IGNATIA GAVIN

Sr. Ignatia Gavin, csa **(1889-1966)**, friend of Alcoholics Anonymous co-founders Bill Wilson and Dr. Bob Smith, helped innumerable alcoholics in her roles as hospital admitting clerk and nun.

Mary C. Darrah tells the story in *Sister Ignatia: Angel of Alcoholics Anonymous*.

Born Della Mary Gavin in Ireland, she learned from her strict Catholic mother than alcoholism was a moral failing: "such a grievous offense against the good God that no one should ever mention the word [drunk]."

She moved to the U.S., entered the Sisters of Charity of St. Augustine and, after teaching music for ten years, developed a nervous condition. When St. Thomas Hospital opened in Akron, Ohio, on September 28, 1928, she was put in charge of the registration desk in the admitting office.

And as an adult, exposed to thousands of those suffering from alcoholism, she revised her childhood view.

At the time alcohol abusers were deemed moral derelicts, beyond the reach of medical care. Though Sr. Ignatia had no formal nursing or medical training, she came to believe that alcoholics are ill—physically, mentally, spiritually. In 1934, she befriended Thomas Scuderi, M.D., an emergency room intern who was sympathetic to her views, and convinced him to allow alcoholics to "rest" in the hospital before sending them back to the streets. Their efforts were rudimentary by today's standards. Dr. Scuderi dosed the alcoholic patients with morphine, while Sr. Ignatia laid on calming hands, then retired to pray in the hospital chapel.

In 1935, Alcoholics Anonymous was born in Akron, co-founded by Bill Wilson and St. Thomas's own Dr. Robert ("Bob") Smith.

At the urging of Dr. Bob, himself a sober alcoholic, on August 16, 1939 (some accounts say August 16, 1935), Sr. Ignatia admitted St. Thomas's first alcoholic patient with a label of "acute gastritis." It is widely agreed that St. Thomas thus became the first hospital in the world to treat alcoholism as a medical condition.

In 1952, Sr. Ignatia was transferred to Cleveland's St. Vincent Charity Hospital where she helped establish an alcoholic ward called the Rosary Hall Solarium. Sr. Ignatia saw to it that the Solarium become a mecca for recovering alcoholics and their families and friends. She worked tirelessly there until her retirement thirteen years later.

According to Darrah, "Fifteen thousand alcoholics overcame their addiction under her direct care. An additional sixty thousand coalcoholic family members are estimated to have benefitted from her healing."

Sr. Ignatia passed away in 1966. Well-wishers, mourners, and media swarmed her Cleveland funeral.

As John Cuthbert Ford, SJ, noted in the Foreword to Darrah's *Sister Ignatia*:

> *"The basic ingredient of quality sobriety is one of spiritual surrender to this spiritual illness and recovery through the spiritual values so exemplified in Sister Ignatia's life... Since the spiritual quality of her mission transcends time, her message is now preserved for all future generations of recovering people."*

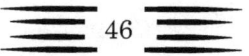

46

ROBERT BRESSON

Robert Bresson (1901-1999), acclaimed French film-maker, used Catholicism, his early calling as a painter, and his experiences as a prisoner-of-war to produce such cinematic masterpieces as *Diary of a Country Priest*, *A Man Escaped*, and *Pickpocket*.

Bresson favored stars with no previous on-screen experience, preferring to call his actors "models." He strictly controlled their actions, down to the number of steps and eye movements.

"The things one can express with the hand, with the head, with the shoulders!" he wrote in *Notes on Cinematography*. "How many useless and encumbering words then disappear."

His working habits were idiosyncratic and uncompromising. He made only 13 features over the space of 40 years.

Loss of innocence, childhood suffering stemming from abusive authority figures, and the seeming absence of God are Bresson's major themes. His films are spare, slow, and allegorical.

Diary of a Country Priest (1951), based on the well-known Georges Bernanos novel, is the tale of a small-town novice priest who fails in almost every particular. Suffering secretly from stomach cancer, and unable to eat anything more than dry bread soaked in wine, he is accused by his parishioners of being a drunk. He tries desperately to help deliver a female parishioner from spiritual peril; the parishioner's young daughter spreads scandalous rumors. And yet as he lays dying, his last words are "All is grace."

Claude Laydu played the curé and was selected, as was true generally of Bresson's actors, not so much for his theatric ability as for the sensitivity and asceticism of his face.

A Man Escaped (1956), shot almost entirely in a lone prison cell, attains almost unbearable existential and religious tension with the sparing use of voice-over and lingering shots of objects and body parts: a bedspring, a hand, a waist.

Au Hasard Balthazar (1966) features a broken-down donkey, and the abused young girl who cares for him, as Christ figures. In *Robert Bresson: A Passion for Film*, Tony Pipolo observed of the film that "The action in the prologue is not primarily conveyed through expositional dialogue, but through gesture, look, and action in succession." Critic Daryl Chin observed that, with his Balthazar cinematographer Ghislain Cloquet, "Bresson would evolve a cinematic style of subtle, sun-dappled radiance; without extending the photography into extremes of chiaroscuro contrast, Cloquet would heighten the lighting so that even the greys would glisten."

Mouchette, Bresson's next work with Cloquet, would, like all his previous films, be in black-and-white. His last five were in color.

Though sometimes described as a "Christian atheist," Bresson observed:

> *"There is the feeling that God is everywhere, and the more I live, the more I see that in nature, in the country.* When I see a tree, I see that God exists. I try to catch and to convey the idea that we have a soul and that the soul is in contact with God. That's the first thing I want to get in my films."

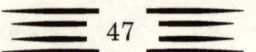

SERVANT OF GOD
LÉONIE MARTIN

Léonie Martin (1863-1941), "difficult" sister of St. Thérèse of Lisieux, failed three times at religious life before succeeding .

The Martin family—mother Zélie, father Louis, and their five daughters—was deeply pious.

The other four Martin sisters were intelligent, lively, charming, quick. Léonie, the middle child, by contrast had few natural graces. Unruly and rebellious, she was expelled from school, suffered from eczema, and occupied the smallest bedroom at Les Buissonets, the family home. Even her own mother referred to her as "poor Léonie."

In 1886, Léonie entered the Poor Clare convent at Alençon, in what would be the first of three attempts at religious life. The rule was rigorous, and owing to poor health, she lasted only six weeks. In 1887, she entered the Visitation

Monastery in the city of Caen. She was forced to leave less than six months later, again due to poor health. She made her second attempt to enter the Visitation at Caen in 1893 and left two years later.

Meanwhile, her younger sister Thérèse had entered the Carmelite convent. The letters she sent to Léonie while there were a great source of consolation, guidance, and support.

Thérèse died of TB in 1897. In 1899, at the age of 35, Léonie again entered the Monastery of the Visitation at Caen. In 1900 she at last became a professed member, taking the name Sister Françoise-Thérèse. She followed the path of the "little way" developed by Thérèse, whom she considered her spiritual mentor.

Léonie lived at Caen for 41 years, until her death at the age of 78, continuing during much of that time to suffer ill health.

She was obscure in life and, eclipsed by her much beloved and world-renowned sister saint, obscure in death. Then, around 1960, prayer requests began coming in to the monastery, directed toward Léonie. People identified with her isolation within the family, her difficulty in finding her vocation, her brokenness, the life of prayer that at last allowed her to transform, rather than transmit, her childhood wounds.

Maureen O'Riordan, keeper of the Léonie Martin website, reports of her tomb: "On the altar in the crypt, a book of intentions. One cannot leaf through it without moistening it with some tears, at the reading of supplications of parents in suffering, rendered powerless by the chaotic itineraries of certain of their children, or of young people in crisis who have trouble finding their way."

Léonie's cause for beatification was opened in 2015. Already she is an unofficial patron of all "black sheep"—and of all parents of black sheep, which is surely a special cross all its own.

Biblical scholar Anne Marie Pelletier notes that, far from detracting from the sanctity of the Martin family, Léonie and her troubles brought a credibility that might otherwise have been lacking. "[T]he Christian life is not an athletic performance!" she observes. "The true Christian life is always a matter of poverty offered to God and transfigured by Him!"

48

GEORGES ROUAULT

Georges Rouault (1871-1958), French Expressionist,
is considered one of the most notable Christian artists of
the twentieth century. His paintings include "Christ on the
Outskirts," "The Crucifixion," and "The Old King."

R ouault grew up in the Belleville quarter on the outskirts
of Paris. "In the *faubourg* of toil and suffering, in
the darkness, I was born," he later wrote. "Keeping vigil
over pictorial turpitudes, I toiled miles away from certain
dilettantes."

His father was a cabinetmaker, and Rouault's first job was as
an artisan's assistant to a restorer of stained glass windows.
"My time there was short, but it marked me with a seal
that was legendary, epical," he said. Ever after he would
remember the spirit of the anonymous medieval artists
who had crafted the glorious windows but refrained from
attaching their names to their work.

In 1891 Rouault painted "The Way to Calvary".

In 1908 he married Marthe Le Sidaner; they had four children.

As early as 1913, one critic, Gustave Coquiot, exclaimed, "One must be a monk to understand him."

Rouault was deeply affected by the outbreak and aftermath of WWI. He became friends with the notoriously irascible Catholic writer Léon Bloy, and later with the philosopher Jacques Maritain and his wife Raïssa, both converts.

He painted fugitives, clowns, prostitutes, beggars and corpses—the casualties of war, materialism, and a complacent bourgeoisie. But Rouault's work was human rather than "political."

As Raïssa Maritain observed, "The quality of a work does not depend on its subject, but on its spirit." Jacques Maritain noted, "This kind of 'realisim' is in no way a realism of physical appearances; it is realism of the spiritual significance of what exists (and moves and suffers and loves and kills); it is realism permeated with the signs and dreams that are commingled with the being of things."

Rouault's masterpiece is widely considered to be the series of mixed-media intaglio prints called *The Miserere*, which he exhibited in 1948. He was close to 80 at the time. With theirs nuanced blacks and grays, the works depict the horror and the sorrow of human suffering, and of every human being's complicity in that suffering. "Are We Not All convicts?" the title of one print asks. Another, of a smug, well-fed man, is entitled "We Think Ourselves Kings." A third, "Street of the Lonely," could with its evocation of existential isolation be the street on which I—or you—live.

The political turmoil, threat of mass destruction, and rise of the right that marked Rouault's era have only intensified in our day. The malady is spiritual and so, as always, is the solution.

In *Rouault: A Vision of Suffering and Salvation*, author William A. Dyrness reports:

"In 1952, a writer for the religious periodical "La Croix" asked Rouault what he thought of religious or sacred art. As usual, Rouault refused to be brought into the debate. He said simply that, to talk about art in the Church, one must first of all love painting."

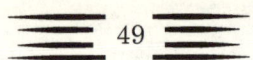 49

JACQUELINE DE DECKER

Jacqueline de Decker (1913-2009), also known as Mother Teresa's "Spiritual Powerhouse," suffered all her adult life from chronic physical pain.

British journalist Kathryn Spink has written beautifully of de Decker and her work in, among other places, *I Need Souls Like You: Sharing in the Work of Mother Teresa Through Prayer and Suffering.*

De Decker was born in 1913 to a wealthy Belgian family. She made her way to India and, in 1947, walked halfway across the country to meet Mother Teresa. Hoping to work with the Missionaries of Charity, instead she was forced back to Antwerp by a chronic, debilitating illness that affected the spine.

De Decker's dream seemed to be smashed. She was devastated.

But in the fall of 1952, she received a letter from Mother Teresa that read in part:

> *"Today I am going to propose something to you. You have been longing to be a missionary. Why not become spiritually bound to our society which you love so dearly? While we*

work in the slums, you share in the prayers and the work with your suffering and your prayers. The work here is tremendous and needs workers, it is true, but I also need souls like yours to pray and suffer."

From among the ranks of fellow patients, de Decker found many people, each of whom was willing to become a "Sick and Suffering Co-Worker" and a link with an individual Missionary of Charity. In turn, Mother Teresa pledged to pray for them.

"By the time I met Jacqueline de Decker her torso was rigidly encased in a corset and her neck was restricted by a surgical collar," Spink writes on her website. "Yet from her home in Antwerp she managed not only to co-ordinate the Link for the sick and suffering, but also to look after the welfare of some 2,000 prostitutes."

On several occasions, Spink accompanied de Decker as she "careened" around Antwerp's red light district in a specially-adapted sports car tending to "her girls."

The experience, Spink observed, brought her "into contact with people suffering from every conceivable illness from elephantiasis to chronic depression. And yet from most, if not all, of these encounters I came away in some unexpected way uplifted."

Mother Teresa came to call de Decker her "sick and suffering self." "By 1980," Spink notes, "Jacqueline had undergone thirty-four operations for her illness, which was never given an official medical label. She called it GGD, or 'God-Given Disease'—her recognition that emptiness, 'failure,' and weakness were the means by which God used her."

De Decker died on April 3, 2009.

"Love demands sacrifice," wrote Mother Teresa. "But if we love until it hurts, God will give us His peace and joy… Suffering in itself is nothing; but suffering joined with Christ's Passion is a wonderful gift."

De Decker's radical apostolate of prayer and self-offering is a model for all of us. Let's pray that our own "God-given diseases" link us as well more closely to the rest of the suffering world.

50

WALKER PERCY

Walker Percy (1916-1990), American novelist whose works include *The Moviegoer* and *Love Among the Ruins*, took as his subject "the dislocation of man in the modern age."

Percy was born in Birmingham, Alabama in 1916. His father committed suicide when the boy was 13. His mother died a few years later after driving her car off a bridge: also, Percy was convinced, a suicide. He and his two brothers were then adopted by his father's first cousin once removed, a gentleman poet who introduced his young charge to many Southern writers. One, Shelby Foote, would remain a lifelong friend.

Percy graduated from Columbia University Medical School in 1941 and contracted TB during his internship. He spent much of his lengthy convalescence reading Dostoevsky and the existential philosopher, Søren Kierkegaard, two writers who would deeply shape his own work. He developed an abiding interest in semiotics, and discovered his vocation as a writer.

Also during that time, he began to recognize the limits of science. Later he would observe, "This life is too much trouble, far too strange, to arrive at the end of it and then to be asked what you make of it and have to answer 'Scientific humanism.' "

In 1946 he married Mary Bernice Townsend, a medical technician. Together the couple converted, and were received into the Church in 1947. They adopted their first child, a daughter, and had another daughter who became deaf while young. The family settled in Covington, Louisiana.

Writing, for Percy, was "a serious business in which the novelist is out both to give joy and to draw blood." Over the course of his career, he authored six novels and over a dozen books of nonfiction.

But his first book, the novel *The Moviegoer* (1961) remains the one for which he is best known. Protagonist Binx Bolling, a New Orleans suburbanite, is the quintessential outsider: alone in a crowd, searching for God in a culture that has been leached of mystery and meaning. Similar to contemporary "binge-watchers," Bolling spends hours alone in darkened cinemas watching films.

In the end, he learns, "There is only one thing I can do: listen to people, see how they stick themselves into the world, hand them along a ways in their dark journey and be handed along, and for good and selfish reasons."

"The thing that fascinates me," Percy told an interviewer in 1971, "is the fact that men can be well-off, judging by their own criteria, with all their needs satisfied, goals achieved, et cetera, yet as time goes on, life is almost unbearable. Amazing!"

He made his final oblation and become a secular oblate at St. Joseph Benedictine Abbey in St. Benedict, Louisiana on February 16, 1990. He died of prostate cancer less than three months later, at 73, and is buried in their cemetery.

Even apart from his books, he should be remembered for one line alone.

He was once asked, apropos of the dogma of the Catholic Church, "How is such a belief possible in this day and age?"

Percy replied: "What else is there?"

Made in the USA
San Bernardino, CA
08 January 2020